Geoff Burch

Writing on the Wall

The campaign for commonsense business

GEOFF BURCH

CAPSTONE

The right of Geoff Burch to be identified as the author of this work has been asserted in accordance with the Copyright, Designs and Patents Act 1988.

First published 2002 by
Capstone Publishing (a Wiley company)
8 Newtec Place
Magdalen Road
Oxford OX4 1RE
United Kingdom
http://www.capstoneideas.com

British Library Cataloguing in Publication Data
A CIP catalogue record for this book is available from the British Library.

ISBN 1-84112-043-X

Typeset in 11/16 pt Palatino by
Sparks Computer Solutions Ltd, Oxford
http://www.sparks.co.uk
Printed and bound by
T.J. International Ltd, Padstow, Cornwall

This book is printed on acid-free paper

Substantial discounts on bulk quantities of Capstone books are available to corporations, professional associations and other organisations. For details telephone Capstone Publishing on (+44-1865-798623), fax (+44-1865-240941) or email (info@wiley-capstone.co.uk).

To my wonderful wife, Sallie, who tries to manage me and protect me from the ravages of the world, and to my sons, and the rest of my loopy barking mad family who drive me nuts and who I love very much

Contents

INTRODUCTION

Some years ago, while being interviewed on radio, I was spouting my usual outrageous opinions on business. After the show I received a mysterious phone call from a sinister individual who asked if I had ever written a book, and if I hadn't, would I like to. I replied no and yes in the correct order, and found myself in a glittering tower, speaking to my future editor who worked for one of the world's biggest publishers. I was overjoyed by the proffered cheque, and overawed by the brief: 'We want an iconoclastic look at business.'

As my wife and I drove away, I was euphoric with the aforementioned cheque in my pocket. My wife, whom I work with, was worried however. 'Money', I mumbled. 'Money.'

'You have never written anything in your life, you can't write,' she said. 'Anyway, what does iconoclastic mean?'

Now there's a point. What does iconoclastic mean? According to the dictionary, an iconoclast is 'one who assails cherished beliefs'.

A recipe for disaster if ever I saw one, but the fact was that I was not that much au fait with businesses' cherished beliefs, anyway. My field was business persuasion, sales, customers, negotiation and all that sort of thing. I wrote about what I knew, and the result was *Resistance is Useless*, a book that is quite iconoclastic for most people and which did very well in any event, but then the weird stuff began to happen. As a result of writing the book, and its attendant publicity, I became bounced into the world of business guru-ship. There was the lecture and conference circuit, a bit of telly and, most astonishing of all, invitations to lecture at prestigious business schools. My title, the Alternative Business Guru! And now, after a few years of guru-ing, I think I am ready, so here is the real iconoclastic look at business.

ARMING THE PEASANTS

– A VERY RISKY BUSINESS INDEED

It is very difficult to know where to start, because at first sight it would be easy to say that nothing works. It would astonish you to learn that virtually every retailer, car dealer, bank, airline, holiday company – or whatever – spends millions on customer care and sales training, but we can all plainly see that their staff and service are crap. Are they mad? Are we mad? They have customer service departments that just provoke us to a frenzy of frustration.

There is an orgy of quality programmes that are a complete waste of time. An aluminium company I know had 30 per cent of its products rejected 20 years ago. Now it has achieved ISO 9001, through TQM (total quality management), and has a quality manager who belongs to the International Institute of Quality Thingys and trails off to their conference every year to re-affirm his beliefs. They now get 31 per cent of the product rejected. Ha!

THOUGHT

It might be fun doing it, but what is the point if it doesn't work?

WHY?

We have salespeople who don't sell, drivers that don't deliver, and promises that are not kept. Why are companies torturing themselves with all this stuff if it doesn't work? What is the point? You may feel that they undertook all these programmes in an attempt to find a more profitable and easy way of working. In other words, to find a way of making more money, but that doesn't seem to be the case. When asked 'Why are you doing this? Why set these targets?' the reply is often bluster and jargon. They don't know why they are doing it.

While we are on the subject of jargon, let's have a list. Empowerment, re-engineering, TQM, *kaizen*, change management, customer focus, benchmarking, bandwidth, flat organisations, no-blame culture, and responsiveness, to name but a tiny fraction.

In my presentations, I like to think that I use a little humour to make points. This tends to outrage the anally retentive who feel that I am adding levity to a very serious subject. Similarly the more advanced a business book is the more difficult, it is believed, it should be to read.

SIMPLE MINDS

Because I am a very simple minded person, I intend to make this a very simple book to read. I admire Handy, Peters, Drucker and Hammer. Their messages can be useful, but by the time the international consultants have turned their thinking into reports with a few charts and graphs, the whole thing is beyond normal human understanding. So, in my defence I would suggest that as most companies employ and sell to normal human beings, doing anything beyond their understanding is utterly useless. I know that those nice people in human resources will translate it all for us simple minded creatures, but like all written words of lore since the Bible, translation is a dicey business. Think about it in medieval Europe, when a monk was translating the New Testament for the monarch, and he came to the bit about red hot pokers being inserted in kings: do you really think he translated that part? When HR gets to the 'why we no longer need HR' document, would they willingly share that information out?

To understand all these trends and theories, and to try and make them work where they didn't, I had to simplify them, and that is what this book will try and do. I promise you that making things simple is very hard to do, and implementing things simply can be very complicated indeed. So forgive me if this book is easy to read, but don't let that devalue it. I am, in my own way, very serious and quite a fanatic, so let us risk a little iconoclasticism that might just lead us all to making lots more money with a bit less stress.

EMPOWERMENT, THE GREAT LIE

The title of this chapter, as you will have gathered, is 'Arming the Peasants', so perhaps an explanation for that is needed as it may be the inspiration for the book. The word that started the whole thing was EMPOWERMENT. A great buzz word and one that is used freely amongst management, but what does it mean? That was not a rhetorical question. Before going on, be completely clear in your mind what your definition is. Like all the great management words, it has lost its value through overuse. In fact, it lost its meaning – that is, if it ever had one. I get bosses ringing up and saying: 'Empowerment!'

'Pardon?'

'Empowerment! I want you to empower my staff!'

'Empowered to do what?'

'To feel empowered to move this company forward into the new millennium through empowerment.'

'Empowered to do what?'

'Erm, empowered to feel empowered.'

'To do what?'

'Erm, empowered, empowered to do what they're told. Yes, that's it, empowered to do what they're told. I want you to empower some discipline into them!'

I used to gently explain that wasn't what I believed empowerment to be.

'You see, I think that empowerment is about moving the decision-making process into the front line, down the food chain, so that your lowliest and cutting-edge staff are able to make executive decisions.'

'How does that help?'

'It keeps customers, it finds customers, it makes money, it saves money.'

On one occasion, the guy I was speaking to was the chief executive of a carpet company and at the mention of the word 'money' his little piggy eyes lit up.

'Money! Tell me about money!'

'Well, take the very bottom element of your company, the carpet fitters. They have the most customer contact, and therefore most customer impact. Imagine the scene when we have empowered them:

> *Customer – 'Excuse me, there seems to be some difference in the pattern.'*
> *Fitter – 'Oh gosh, you're right, I am so terribly sorry. You must be so disappointed. What would you like me to do?'*
> *Customer – 'What can you do?'*
> *Fitter – 'Anything. I can do anything you like.'*
> *Customer – 'A refund?'*
> *Fitter – 'Certainly. How much – £50?'*
> *Customer – '£50 would be great.'*

With that, the fitter will pull out a bundle of notes, and count out ten £5 notes.

> *Fitter – '£50 – now are you sure you are happy with that?'*
> *Customer – 'Yes, delighted.'*

I smile in anticipation of praise at my brilliant analysis.

'You're a loony.'

'Pardon?'

'You're a complete loony. Are you seriously suggesting that we give our fitters cash?'

'Yes. What's the problem?'

'They'd bugger off with it, that's the problem, they would clear off to the bookies before you could wink.'

'What sort of people are you employing?'

'The sort of people that would bugger off with our cash, that's who. How can that save us money? It will cost us money.'

'But look what's happening now!' I cried.

Customer – 'There seems to be a slight difference in the pattern.'

Fitter – 'Not surprised.'

Customer – 'Why?'

Fitter – 'These carpets are crap – buggers to fit too, if you think the pattern's funny, you wait till it starts to smell!'

Customer – 'SMELL! What are you going to do about it?'

Fitter – 'Can't do anything – got ten more of these things to fit. You'll have to ring the office.'

Customer Service – 'Thank you for ringing Happy Pile Carpets. Can I point out that a carpet is a naturally woven product and you can expect some differential in pattern and colour, and if you're unhappy with that, tough!'

POINT

Empowerment may seem a dangerous idea, but if your people can handle things quickly, disaster is often avoided and wonderful, profitable things happen.

The customer at this point can do a selection of things, but all are bad for business. They might vanish forever, or they could tenaciously start to percolate up through the organisation. With each rejection, they gather ire like some infernal snowball until they reach the top, by which time their demands have grown: "I WANT A FREE HOUSE FROM YOU!"

A BAD ATTITUDE

Now before we move on, I think we need to examine this situation more closely.

I sometimes use this tale to entertain audiences at conferences, and they laugh because they can give knowing nods about the behaviour of their own fitters, drivers or whatever. What I am trying to do, I suppose, is to show that despite the risks, genuine empowerment is the only way to go, but that is very easy for me to say. If we dismantle the story, it becomes truly complicated and, I suppose, the driving force for this book.

The first point to think about is ATTITUDE.

Why on earth did the fitter say his company's produce was 'crap'? Is he mad? He is damaging the company that pays him, but it is a classic situation. If we worked in a meat pie factory, there is one thing we would never eat. 'Don't eat one of those – I work there. I know what goes on. We lost a rat the other day, I swear it went in the chicken and mushroom!'

Why do people do that? We have all done it. Do we stand around the photocopier and say: 'This is the finest company in the world and I intend to strive, through my simple effort, to make it better'? Well, you don't say that if you want to avoid a kicking from your colleagues.

I have noticed recently that a few business books have used Dilbert cartoons to give a wry insight into management, but despite them being very funny I hate the Dilberts of this world. Dilbert is lazy, disloyal and seditious.

Tip number one – Sack your Dilberts.

The first battle, then, is for the attitude of the entire team. We will deal with this whole subject later but just as a teaser, ask yourself: right from the start, when you recruit are you looking for attitude or skill? If you don't actively look for a good attitude, then people are very unlikely to suddenly develop one.

ALL YOUR PEOPLE SHOULD BE WORKING TOGETHER TO MOVE THE COMPANY FORWARD.

But where to? Do people understand what the company's ambitions are? This brings us to the second problem, and that is of the confusing messages we give out to our people. Again, a subject for much more discussion later, but for now how do we set, measure and reward this fitter's work? We also need to consider the problem that originally drove the working practices. Maybe they only fitted four carpets a day and, by introducing a bonus scheme, we were able to raise that to ten. What was the priority here? I know this is the old piecework chestnut, but let's take a slightly different look at it. More than the piecework thing, the biggest threat is that the fragmented component divisions of a company all have different objectives, goals and priorities, that can often damage the goals and priorities of the other departments. I suppose this brings us back to Point One, which is that we should all be working for the same goal. Simple.

As an old hippy, I would call this the holistic approach. The Islington trendies call it joined-up government, and Hammer calls it process re-engineering. Process re-engineering is a simple, elegant way to make a company streamlined, productive, and efficient. When you read books on it you think that it looks easy. You do it, and it doesn't work. To get my head round the carpet fitter problem, and the intricacies of re-engineering, I needed to develop a much simpler model that would fit my much simpler mind. So, instead of all the complexities of a modern company, I have decided to go back to a simpler time.

COME BACK WITH ME

Consider the situation of a medieval Baron. The old Baron has died, and the young zesty son has inherited a hell of a mess. It is interesting to note that the hell of a mess thing is often only noticed when there is some kind of dynastic change. Perhaps we are happier living with our own mess than going to all the uproar of changing it. Anyway, I digress. The new Baron is horrified at what he finds. There are weird arcane practices, strange hierarchies, bizarre rituals and hundreds of priests, soothsayers and minor Lords. Worst of all, shed loads of money is haemorrhaging out of his coffers. None of his internal advisers give honest advice because they jealously guard their own sinecures. There is no choice but to call in the medieval equivalent of consultants, which in this case is Machiavelli and Co. After taking a nice fat learning curve fee, they suggest that things cannot progress without a full staff audit. This agreed, they set about conducting one, and soon return with the results and another large bill.

'We've found your problem,' they say while capering gleefully around. 'There are just too many people, what you need is a bit of process re-engineering. Look, you've got your peasants – that's where all your production comes from, growing the crops, herding the cows; OK, there's the blacksmith – makes all sort of useful bits and bobs, and with maintenance jobs, he's worth having around. There's the miller, grinding corn, making bread, you can see the point of him. But when you get to the castle (or head office as we call it), well what a state, there are ladies in waiting, marketing, knights, alchemists, accountants, soothsayers and sages. Get rid of the lot. What this will give you is the classic flat organisation.'

'Flat organisation, how does that work?'

'Beautifully. It's simple – peasants work, you gather profit. Two levels – peasant/baron. Baron/peasant. No middle.' (By the way, reader, you can put yourself anywhere you like in this model.)

'The peasants work, I get the money?'

'Yep.'

It's not long before the Baron's shiny new flat organisation is up and running. Costs are slashed, production is up and the Baron is rich and happy, but a cloud is gathering. The still inefficient but aggressive Baron from next door eyes our third way Baron with a greedy glint. He hasn't laid off his knights and men at arms because although a very expensive and ill-used resource, armies can be useful when fighting. In fact they are only useful when fighting which I suppose begs the philosophical question does supporting an army tend to make you want to fight more, and do acquisitive companies have to keep making acquisitions, just to justify themselves?

Anyway, the wicked Baron has been massing his army on our hero's border. The young Baron views the scene with horror, and scampers back to Machiavelli and Co.

'Great idea your flat organisation. I'm going to get a right kicking now.'

'I wouldn't worry, you're still a much bigger organisation than he is, you've got far more people and land than he has.'

'Yes, I know that, but it's all production and peasants. Haven't you ever heard of a leverage buyout?'

'You've got a point, we'll have to go away and think about this.'

'Don't be long.'

A few days later the consultants are back, breathless and excited.

'We solved it. The classic solution in re-engineered and flattened organisations.'

'That is?'

'Multi-tasking. What your peasants need is a spot of multi-tasking.'

'Explain.'

'You should arm the peasants.'

'Arm the peasants, are you mad? You're a loony.' (I'm getting a bit of déjà vu here). 'You are seriously suggesting that I give my peasants GUNS?'

'Yep, anything wrong with that?'

'Sure is. If I give my peasants guns, the first person they'll shoot is me. They hate me.' (Just the way fitters will bugger off with cash.)

'You've got a point. Leave it with us.'

A short time later the consultants are back, and they can hardly contain their excitement. 'Boy, oh boy, we have got it sorted now. What you do is Arm the Peasants. You can give them guns, but then you don't give them ammunition. To the world they will appear armed, but we know that they can be of no real danger.' So there we have it. 'Arming the Peasants' explains a lot of strange goings on.

I stayed at one of those motorway stops where the money is taken from your credit card when you go in. You get a reasonably clean room, shower and TV, but if you want food it is sent from the motorway services along with all the attendant service area quality problems, i.e., a pizza that is like a Frisbee with tepid vomit glued to it with rubber cement. Oh well, that's what you pay for, that's what you get, and anyway there is no human to complain to – they've got your money so 'c'est la vie'. Until one day I was leaving one of these places, followed by my fellow 'guests', when a thing dressed in a bilious-coloured suit leapt out and said 'I'm Tracey, your hostess. Thank you for staying at Gulag Inn, could I ask you if everything was OK with your stay?'

'Ah, no. My pizza tasted like a Frisbee with tepid vomit glued to it.'

She stared at me with a look of growing panic and confusion, her lips moving on auto-pilot, but no sound came. Obviously someone had pressed a hidden reset button, because her eyes blinked, she regained her composure, and looked past me to the man behind. 'I'm Tracey, your hostess. Thank you for staying at Gulag Inn, could ...' An unarmed peasant if ever I saw one. She looked armed, but had no ammunition.

THINK ABOUT THIS

You may think this tale makes some kind of profound observation, which I will then take as a learning point, but it isn't that easy. I am not entirely sure what is learned, or what point I am making. In my most depressed state, which I will be in a later chapter, I may suggest that customer care is (in this sort of company) stone dead and, in any case, offers little benefit. The old saying I used to churn out of finding and keeping customers being the only profitable activity of any company has become a little devalued now, and to be frank, companies like this couldn't care less. They also know that tired, dispirited punters will trail back to them to suffer horrid food and zero service because this is the 'benchmark' for roadside service and, anyway, those that dare to take a packed lunch and sleep in their cars will be replaced by lemming-like hordes of fresh fodder for their mill. Also, while we are at it, the staff are systematically crap, disloyal, disinterested, and basically untrainable beyond simply walking upright and not fiddling with personal orifices when preparing food in view or speaking to a customer. They are the sort of people who would bugger off with the cash, and there may not be anything better on offer.

Why bother?

So why bother teaching the lumpen thing the speech anyway? Maybe it shows a commitment to some attempt at good service. No, it doesn't. In actual fact it is pulling a trick that dear old Mother Nature has been using for years, and that is that an unarmed peasant works until it has been rumbled. For example, there is a completely harmless, unarmed but very tasty butterfly, that when its wings are spread, presents a pattern that looks like the eyes of a fierce animal many times the butterfly's size. This works extremely well, putting off most predators. Similarly most customers do not tenaciously test the veneer of useless promises (I'm Tracey, I'm here to help). The whole thing falls on its arse when the predator is hungry enough to give it a go, and finds a yummy, unprotected morsel. Word gets around, and soon there is a species of frog that dines entirely off our ingenious chum.

You know who

Our own high street giants have fallen prey to this. For years, people have come up to me and asked me to do a bit of guru-ing for them, with the brief 'We want service levels like you-know-who on the High Street.'

'Why? They're rubbish, their service is rubbish, they have total contempt for staff and punters alike.' (Actually contempt suggests passion, indifference would be a better word.) The shock this statement used to cause was comic, you would think they had been slapped.

'You can't say that.'

'Tell me about their great service.'

'Well, um, they give great service, if you want something they haven't got, they, er well, there is always someone to er, they, they, er, don't mind if er, well you can always take stuff back. I took something back, they gave me another one.'

'Why did you take it back?'

'Because the wheels fell off, but even if it's the wrong size you can take it back.'

'Why didn't you try it there?'

'There wasn't actually anywhere to try it.'

But then – snap, they took a bite, the shares started to tumble, the feeding frenzy started, and the game was up.

CONCLUSION

Unarmed peasants is a truly good scam, as long as no one calls their bluff.

While we are back at the peasants, what did I want the girl to do? Again, like the carpet fitter, a cash refund might have been nice (no, not vouchers or discount off my next stay). 'I'm so sorry you were disappointed. Please let me refund the cost of your meal. We would hate to lose you as a customer.' And, with a couple of crisp tenners in my pocket, the world would have seemed a better place.

That may seem ideal and a simple solution but, as previously stated, simple things become fiendishly complicated on implementation.

Let us imagine that we have helpful, loyal staff who could use judgement and be trusted to handle cash responsibly. Thus whenever a customer received a poor meal, they could be delighted with a cash refund.

'Oh no!' the service area owners wail. 'The food is consistently horrible, everyone would get a refund, we would be ruined!'

Then (and now we get into deep water) the 'hostess' should feel aggrieved at having to give money away, and should go to the kitchens and be able to command the construction of a better pizza.

'She has no authority in the kitchen.'

'She should have.'

'She can't, she's a simple peasant, cannon fodder.'

'Now look here, I get pissed off with having my complaint fielded by powerless peasants.'

There's the rub. Even when companies have large (I was going to say sophisticated, but I couldn't hold the pen for laughing) customer service departments, they cannot actually change the product or the policy of the company. This is quite clearly a ludicrous state of affairs which upsets and humiliates the customers when they realise that only platitudes and vouchers are coming their way, and that nothing has really changed.

If we return for a moment to our Baron, imagine you were in his situation and felt that the idea of the unarmed peasant bluff was not worth risking. Other options have to be considered. The first is that of using outside talent; after all, this whole thing was started off by consultants. Why not continue the process? As it has already been stated that armies are only useful when fighting wars, then surely it would be sensible to find a company whose sole business was fighting? They could devote their resources, training and equipment to the subtle art of killing people. I get confused, because at the start of my business awareness everyone was shouting 'Diversify.' Now they are shouting 'Stick to the knitting, stay with what you know.' I saw a television programme on business where a catering company was trying to sell its services to an insurance company.

'What's your business?'

'Insurance.'

'How much is your training budget?'

'25 million.'

'How much of that is devoted to training people in how to select and prepare soft fruit?'

'Don't be stupid, none. We're an insurance company.'

'Precisely. Eight per cent of our training budget went on our soft fruit programme. The other 92 per cent was all food and hygiene related. Why on earth are you messing about employing your own catering staff?'

GAME, SET AND MATCH? BUT ...

What we are really talking about here is hiring mercenaries (HIRING CONSULTANTS IS JUST LIKE HIRING MERCENAR-

IES. WHICHEVER ONE I HAPPEN TO BE TALKING ABOUT, AMUSE YOURSELF BY DRAWING THE ANALOGY BETWEEN THE TWO). No one hires cheap mercenaries – well, no one who subsequently doesn't regret it. You hire them by reputation and you don't save money by hiring the second fastest gun, because your opponent only needs to hire the first fastest. We must ask ourselves how they got that fast, and the answer is fighting for others. Where is the future career for them? Again, fighting for others (hopefully not for your enemy, but of course it will be, because it is your sphere of business they understand). I make my living from consultancy. I am a hired gun, and I gather all my insights and experience from previous clients. When you choose your mercenary/consultant, you don't want the hair-trigger 24-year-old MBA. You want the Yul Brynner, the man in black with a few scars, a piece of ear missing, well used guns, a black hat, and eyes like steel bearings. Be warned, you only control him while you pay him. When you stop, he could, without emotion, become your enemy's hired gun. Marketing companies, research outfits, direct mail, lawyers, PR companies and management consultancies all work on this principle. I would never profess to be clever, but I have gathered knowledge, like a bee gathers nectar, from a thousand companies. This is the deal. You pay for the value of this experience, but part of the fee is that you are also contributing experience that can be used on the next assignment – useful for a short time, but also expensive. Then, maybe, the hired gun could teach the peasants to fight (watch *The Magnificent Seven* to see how this is done).

This, the Baron thinks, is the right course of action and the consultants return. The first problem to solve is why the peasants want to shoot the Baron, or why they don't seem to care if they are invaded but, after all, being enslaved to another vicious, heartless git is no different from being enslaved to the current one. Why do employees steal, disparage the company and produce poor quality goods? Perhaps because they are seen as peasants. Finance departments always put them on the liability, not the asset side of the books. Short of work? Cut staff.

Companies just do things without consultation, and then they wonder why the peasants didn't buy in with unbounded enthusiasm. We therefore need to explore how we get that buy-in without resentment. Later, we will see how to achieve that essential change in attitudes.

The Baron, in the meantime, does all the trendy third-way things and retitles the peasants as stakeholders. He then launches a hearts and minds campaign that makes the peasa ... – sorry, stakeholders – love him. They also see that as stakeholders they now have a vested interest in protecting the baronial lands, or should we say stakeholderdom. Let's now take stock. We have a team that is loyal, loves and respects their leaders, and wants to work for what they now acknowledge as the common good. This is looking great. Do you think this may be the time to arm them? Yes?

Can you imagine a bunch of enthusiastic peasants let loose with modern battlefield weapons? All hell would be let loose. They would shoot themselves in the feet, you in the arse, and all with the best possible motives. I'm sure you are now one step ahead of me, and will suggest that training is required. The carpet fitter is the same. If he loves the company and respects the products, and is scrupulously honest, could he still, in real terms, be responsible for your refunds policy? With enough training you can turn your peasants into a finely honed fighting machine – an army, which kind of takes us back to square one. Truthfully it is even more dangerous than that. What you have actually got is a vicious fighting force that will do agricultural work for you because they love and trust you. Betray that trust, speak with forked tongue, nick their rations, and it will be hanging from a lamp-post by your heels time. In the real world it is a risk most firms don't feel is worth taking, but when attacked by the fanatics who are their competitors, they have no defence. The 'monster/butterfly' trick doesn't work because they would have attacked the monster, dangerous or not. They believe that there is nothing better than to die in the jaws of a slavering blood beast for the glorious leader, and worse, when they find out we are bluffing, we are quickly overwhelmed.

So there it is, arming the peasant and all its attendant difficulties. It is hard and dangerous if you do it – fatal if you don't. Hopefully in the next few chapters we will explore how it can be done with the least risk.

The benefit will be not only loyal, hard-working people, which a lot of firms claim to have, but people that actively promote the company they work for. People that don't only keep current customers but actively help to find new ones. Every accountant, salesman, driver, receptionist, engineer and cleaner will understand the overall vision and goal and will work together to achieve it for you. I offer you a fierce, loyal, fighting peasants' army that will give their all to win your battles.

THE PROCESS

Process re-engineering is, or was, a great buzz word a while ago.

To explain, for those of us who have been living in the jungle for the last few years, not knowing that the war was over. The 'process' is not the art of getting great whirling cogwheels to mesh in such an artful way that 50 million halved cherries are placed dead centre on 50 million iced bakewell tarts. No, that is the old, boring, nontrendy, logical description of the process. No, apparently what it now means is the process of the activity of the whole company from marketing, sales, production, through logistics and, to those of you who can suspend a viciously cynical sense of humour, even accounts. Why? To cut bureaucracy, and to streamline and flatten the organisation to the benefit of all – except those who get the chop, of course!

Now, I don't really know where to start, but the whole thing goes tits up fairly quickly on the first golden rule of re-engineering, and that is: 'Everyone is Involved'.

A STUPID BIRD

Many years ago, a bird called the great bustard was believed to be extinct until late one November some were discovered to be alive. A wonderful cartoon appeared which showed hawks in a zoo viewing the new arrival and saying 'I would consider myself a very silly bustard indeed, showing up this near Christmas, looking that much like a turkey' (which the bustard did). By the same token, I would consider a Director who re-engineered himself out of a job a very silly Director indeed.

Ergo: **PROCESS RE-ENGINEERING ONLY APPLIES TO THE LOWER ORDERS**

Some directors derive their power from the size or expertise of the staff in their department – i.e., IT, Accounts or HR. Reduction in department size is tantamount to a surgical reduction in prowess.

Ergo: **SOME DEPARTMENTS CAN BE RING-FENCED**

At its most crude and vicious, process re-engineering is just an excuse for a staff cull. To put it into management euphemism, downsizing and outplacing.

WHY BOTHER?

So what does it mean and why is it so difficult? And if it is difficult, why bother?

The 'why bother' question could be best illustrated by my own experience. A company telephoned and told me that they needed some training because they had a customer care problem. I have been suckered too often to fall into the trap of offering training before being sure the problem actually existed in the way the client saw it. They told me the real trouble lay with the customer interface, namely the people who manned the sales desks. The company in question manufacture a very technical range of pumps, so the sales staff, both internal and external, were in effect sales engineers. I offered to come and watch their sales desk in action to see if I could identify the problem.

Come to think of it, what was the problem? They told me that the customers were getting pissed off with the bad service levels, and that they felt the sales staff were defensive and unhelpful. For a long time I have felt that companies make a big mistake when they employ crap staff, but what makes them crap? There was a TV series recently that followed a budget holiday company. To watch it you would have seen that one of the biggest problems was the surly and defensive staff but when you watched a little longer, it was apparent that the company had contempt for staff and clients alike. The company's money-driven inflexibility would have created bad staff from saints. I deal with these issues elsewhere, but in this case I arrived with a pretty open mind.

I sat for a day or two with a young sales engineer who I felt seemed competent, and cheery enough, but one case in particular threw the whole problem into sharp focus.

THOUGHT

Real trouble starts if a 'paper over the cracks' customer care programme is applied to the gaping wound of a crap process or company culture.

The telephone rang and the voice on the other end of the phone introduced itself as one of their major clients who wanted to place an order for £100,000 worth of pumps. Our chum thanked the client for their valued order and then proceeded to tell him that delivery would take around 14 weeks. At this the client went bonkers. (Why he should have done, I don't know. If he had done business with them before, he should have known delivery was rubbish.) He explained that they were in a desert somewhere with a busted oil well and that every minute cost them thousands. My guy apologised and said he would see what he could do. On putting the phone down, he sat back, shook his head and mumbled 'no chance'.

I asked him what he meant by that. He explained that 14 weeks was over-promising and that the client would be very lucky if they achieved that. I said that I supposed making a pump was a very complicated business from drawing board to pattern making, costing, testing, etc. Although a long time, maybe 14 weeks could be expected, at worst.

He looked at me as though I was mad. 'What do you mean, making a pump? They're here, or at one of our subcontractors, there are no specials in this order, they're all "off the shelf" items.'

'Then what takes 14 weeks?'

'It does.'

'What does?'

'Getting it done, does.'

Now we get to it, he is talking about the 'process', the thief of time. Fourteen weeks spent just cocking about. It's a madness you would think you could put a stop to with the stroke of a pen. Apart from anything else, this is a stonking great factory we are talking about here, where time costs a fortune, fixed costs are often calculated at hundreds of pounds an hour, and we blithely accept 14 weeks' worth of them subtracted from the potential profit of this order. The entire time this blithering and blathering goes on, some useless, time-wasting tin god is being paid a whopping salary for these wasted hours.

SOMETHING TO THINK ABOUT

There was a huge engineering works nearby when I was young, where it was accepted practice to cock things up and work slowly during the week so that weekend overtime could be guaranteed.

AN EXERCISE

*I know I am supposed to be a guru, but I don't have all the answers. How would **you** stop this happening?*

SOMETHING ELSE TO THINK ABOUT

An American friend of mine was astonished to hear that British car mechanics get paid at the end of the week regardless of the success of the repair. The mechanics in his garage only get paid on successful job completion. If the customers bring the car back with a failed repair, the mechanic won't be paid for the remedial work.

THOUGHT

When we hire a self employed person, we ask only for outcome: 'mend my boiler', 'paint my house', 'you have landscaped my garden, how much do you want?' With our own people, we don't give a toss about outcome (in fact some of our people don't even know what the outcome is supposed to be), but we are obsessed with process: 'How did you achieve these figures?' True empowerment can only come by managing outcomes and forgetting processes.

DOWNSIDE: On introduction of such a scheme you are likely to be pursued by hordes of broke, angry, hairy-arsed mechanics all wielding large spanners.

UPSIDE: Quality and right-first-time scores go through the roof.

CONCLUSION: Perhaps we pay people for the wrong reason, paying them to do things we don't want them to do.

YOU NEED A COMPUTER TO REALLY SCREW THINGS UP

Now the word 'process' starts to come into the conversation. The company in question has spent a fortune on IT. Why? I quote: 'to speed up the process'. But it hasn't, so what has it done?

We all feel we are busy, and in modern high-performance business, very, very busy indeed. In fact, to pay people maximum money and still maintain profit, high-quality people must be worked to the limit. So when the propeller heads from IT appear with a huge piece of beige luggage and a thing that looks like a portable TV, saying 'Think you're busy now? Wait till you get a load of this,' it doesn't overwhelm us with happiness or the feeling that mastering this 'new system' is going to make life any easier. In fact it usually makes things more complicated.

Again, we are back to semantics. IT stands for 'Information Technology'. In other words, it is the technology that provides you with information. But one of the classic paranoias of management is the Machiavellian statement that 'knowledge is power'. Share knowledge, share power, and before you know it, we are all wearing Che Guevara berets, holding the thoughts of Mao Tse-tung close to our chests and singing the 'Red Flag'. If you consider that most paper systems were created through a lack of trust.

'Nothing leaves this place without the correct paperwork.'

' 'Ere, Frank, if you're short a few on inventory, swipe a couple from service.'

Then:

'Nothing moves internally without the correct paperwork', 'Not without a signed order, you don't,' 'Got the paperwork, driver?'

I may be taking the mick, but then perhaps having 'trust nobody' as a motto can keep you out of a lot of trouble. The danger is that all this paperwork can grind you to a horrible halt, or at best can extend delivery time to 14 weeks. But wait, here come computers. They can think at the speed of light, that should speed things up. What things? All they do is get you into trouble faster. We have seen the unspeakable trouble Government has got itself into by trying to computerise anything from tax to benefits to air traffic control – speed of light? Speed of snail and cost of billions more like. Are we geniuses? Can we see what the great minds advising government can't see? Well, yes and no. For reasons we are about to see, we must hope that government doesn't adopt the solution to this problem because it all could get very sinister indeed.

SINISTER GOVERNMENT

Luckily for us government and politics attract the stupidest people, because if the road tax computer could tell the income tax computer that you drove a Mercedes, or the TV licence computer mentioned to the family income support department about your second home, you would soon be in the shit. It is called 'joined up' by government, but as they need an atlas to find their arses, you can relax.

What really happens is that people replicate the old paper system on the computer. Now instead of total bollocks, you get virtual bollocks. You've read the invoice, you've seen the purchase order docket book, now see it all in glorious technicolour on TV at a desk near you.

THE GENIE IN THE BOTTLE

The real potential for IT is truly amazing. IT's ability to satisfy customers, find customers, win business, replace stuff and generally do astonishingly brilliant things for your business is virtually unlimited. What is limited is our heads, and the reluctance to unchain the beast. It's like finding a very powerful genie in a bottle and when we peer through the grubby, dark glass to try and ascertain just how powerful, we catch a glimpse of a scale, a claw and a few fangs. The instructions say 'Pull this cork to release full power.' OK, but if it turns nasty, can we get the sodding thing back in the bottle? You know the answer as well as I do. NO.

What we do instead is trundle around using computers in a linear, paperworky sort of way, which actually makes them harder to use than the paper they replace. What they could do I think we should leave to the end of this chapter.

A STOCK ANSWER

Back to our hero who fires up the computer terminal on his desk. Part of the order is one particular type of pump. He calls up his sales parts list. Yes, that's right, sales parts list – that is not the same as internal parts list, stock order or spares parts list, production code number, or the fact that marketing call it the Thunderspeed Pump 4000, despite the fact it's the same part. But no matter. Once the computer has translated the customer's description into the likely possibility that what he wants corresponds to a nineteen-digit stock order code, we're on our way. First chance for the customer to receive the wrong order, but as it is going to take 14 weeks, it is a bit like Schrödinger's Cat. For those of you who are into quantum mechanics, you could express it thus: if there is a mistake in your order, or not a mistake in your order, during the 14-week wait you don't know whether you have the correct order or the incorrect order coming, so we have to say that until you open the package you have both the correct and incorrect components. Setting the whimsy of quantum mechanics aside, this could truly piss you off if after 14 weeks by a busted oil well in a desert you finally got the wrong bit. In fact, Schrödinger's Cat could be firmly inserted in another inaccessible place.

Another bright stunt this company pulled during their 'programme of continuous improvement' was to change a part and keep the *same* number, so that when you got what they described as the right part in the desert, it still wouldn't fit. They just didn't tell anyone of these modifications. That of course is the rub, no one tells anyone anything because of the fear of the Che Guevara beret. (I bet you are starting to guess that improved communications may help, but communications with whom? Answer, everyone, and what modern piece of kit can communicate information to everyone at the speed of light? Mmmmm.)

The cathode ray tube flickers into life, the huge number is typed in and, after a short pause, the modern miracle shows there are a hundred of the items required in stock. We need exactly one hundred. Hurrah. The cursor is clicked on the stock display and the virtual pumps are dragged to the sales position, but as soon as the mouse is released they trundle – with a jolly sort of bleeping gait – back into the stock position. They are dragged back down and then set off, bleeping happily, back up the screen again. Soon anger is driving the mouse and its little rubber ball is shrieking in protest. The whole thing degenerates to a point where it resembles the early ping-pong computer games with this order pinging and ponging diagonally across the screen. Finally the phone rings, and a furious voice shouts 'Warehouse speaking! What's going on with these pumps then?'

My guy replies 'I've sold them.'

'What, all hundred of them?'

'Yes.'

'You can't sell all of them, they're stock!'

ONLY ONE PER CUSTOMER

The ensuing conversation degenerated into a fairly vicious slanging match, but amongst the shouting emerged a sort of cockeyed logic, which suggested that as long as stock was sold in the normal quantities of four or five, or even ten or eleven, then it would last for a predicted period, but if some anarchist screwed up the system by achieving a large order, then that endangered everything. It would be like us going into a supermarket to cater for a barbecue party and buying every watermelon on display, then to have the manager appear and say 'You can't buy them all, there will be none left for anyone else.'

I suppose there is a point there, and sometimes the supermarkets have such great offers that they put up the sign 'only one per customer', but throughout the whole store, on all the stock? In a wonderfully bonkers, 'Alice-in-Wonderlandy' sort of way, when I wryly suggested that this engineering company should put a 'no more than one per customer' warning in their brochure, this storeman decided that this would not be a totally bad idea. 'Save us a lot of trouble, but then you don't realise how sly and conniving customers can be. They would start ringing in twice or more with false names and all sorts. If they want stock, they will always find a way round the rules.'

THOUGHT

Being self-employed and paranoid I hate saying no to an offer of work, even one that is impossible to fulfil, based on the fear that if you turn jobs down you may never work again. But setting this aside, imagine you sell sheepskin liberty bodices, and you are so brilliant and customer focused that just by word of mouth people beat a path to your door. Soon all your stock is sold, and a customer rings up to order, but you have none left. I know you can't fulfil every customer's desire, and sometimes we have to say no, but here is a great dilemma, because the other side of this coin is that here we have a person with cash who wants to give our product or service a try. Our restaurant is booked, we are out of stock, the aircraft is full, or we just don't make them anymore, and there they stand with the money in their hand. All the work we do with marketing, mail shots, sales and customer service, then at the final hurdle we turn them away. To do what? To go and give our competitors a try, and I know you don't want to consider this, but our competition may do a better job and we might never see the customer again.

I went to a weird country cinema once, and they were full for the big film. They saw our disappointment and set up two deckchairs at the back (against every health and safety rule, I am sure). I was thrilled. Do your staff realise this sort of thing works? Do you realise this, and do you all know what to do about it?

THINK BUBBLE

People who ring us. If we are tempted to say 'no', imagine them with a wad of cash in their hand that they will give to our bitterest rival if we can't take it from them. Make sure everyone who is working with you understands this.

A CUNNING PLAN FROM MANAGEMENT

A little time after our telephone run-in with the voice in warehousing, a 'suit' appeared. Striding up to us, he said to my hapless chum 'I've just had a difficult conversation with my opposite number in warehousing. Apparently you have upset one of his staff. If you need to communicate with other divisions, then do it through me.'

The problem was duly explained to the 'suit' who said he would attend to it. Days later, he came back with the solution. The stock pumps were not due for delivery for several weeks as the rest of the order had to be gathered, so they would be left on the shelf and still be counted as stock for the inventory, but they would be ring-fenced and described as reserved for sales. Of course it goes without saying that someone had an 'urgent' order to fill, and took six of the pumps leaving 94. That is why, when you order things, you never get the right number. I decided to get involved, and went off to see what was going on.

If they are short six for the order, then the solution is simple: make six more. The word division is an interesting one. When there is a war brewing somewhere in the world, the terrorists and agitators are accused of creating divisions, derived from the word 'divisive', to disrupt the chances of peace. A bad thing.

As a company grows, they decide to create divisions. A good thing?

This company had created divisions and if I wanted to talk about making pumps, I would need to speak to the production division. 'Will you make some more of these pumps, please?'

'No, they aren't on the schedule. We are not due to tool up for another run of these for nine months.'

'Why not?'

'From our calculations, we don't need to.'

'You do need to!'

'No we don't, the computer clearly shows we have a hundred in stock.'

THE ITALIAN JOB

I am often accused of wild exaggeration to make my point, but in this case, apart from subtly removing real names to avoid litigation, every word of the above is true. In fact, worse was to come, because an outside supplier was to contribute 20% of this order. Let's call him Big Tony in Naples, where the order was phoned through.

'Hey, my friend, lovely to hear from you – 250 pumps – my pleasure. Urgent for July? Sure. Ciao.'

My friend put the phone down with a look of misery. I told him he should look happy. The pumps would be with him in three or four weeks. He gave me a look of pity for the poor simple-minded idiot that I was.

'They are Italian, they all bugger off for the whole month of August.'

'But they promised delivery before August.'

His reply was a silent, pursed-lip gaze that made me shrink inside. I didn't push it any further, but sure enough there was no sign of these pumps by mid-September. Our chum finally cracked and he tore into friend Tony, who had completely and cheerfully disregarded the order, the deadline, and any sense of urgency. The row was heated, vicious, and short, but it generated an almost instant reaction in the shape of the 'suit' swiftly bearing down on us.

'Listen! Now you have upset a supplier! And you!' he frothed, stabbing a bony digit in my direction, 'You are supposed to be training *that* kind of behaviour out of him. You get this straight, you communicate through the correct channels. It is not up to you to bollock suppliers. If anyone is going to communicate with suppliers, it will be purchasing. You should have gone through purchasing in the first place. Now they are up in arms. If every snotty salesman could order goods direct, where would that leave purchasing? You will communicate through me to the appropriate divisions, or else.' With the threat left floating in the air like post-Vindaloo flatulence, he stormed off.

THE POINT

My wife, who works closely with me (she locks me in my office even on sunny days to write these books, then is viciously critical of them when I do) tends to say, when reading one of my tirades, 'So what, what is the point and what should people do about it?'

The first thing to note is the dangerous ground this company is on. Not just for their awful work practices, because they have always been awful. Awful work practices or processes have rarely made a dent in western industry until recently. Then the double whammy of the global market and fast communications start sifting through inefficient companies. In our section on change, I will re-boil Charles Handy's frog, but suffice it to say that for now, the survivors haven't noticed the death of their chums.

A CHEERY SAYING
Its not the big that eat the small, but the fast that eat the slow.

If you look at the wild, that statement is very true. The huge wildebeest is hauled down and torn to bits by the speeding cheetah, but even more scary is the reaction of the other wildebeest. Sure, they scamper about in terror whilst the big cat selects its prey, but once the throat is bitten and eating commences, they all go calmly back to grazing. 'I see Frank's being eaten by cheetahs.'

'Aye, Terry, 'appens to the best of us.'

'Sad days, sad bleedin' days.'

Now I would be howling about in terror and would get as far away as possible from anything fast and spotty. Yet companies are like wildebeest, the gory disembowelling of their chums just leaves more grass for them.

The people in the subject company hold up their continuing prosperity as a counter to my criticism, but they are successful despite their process, not because of it. They manufacture a specialist industrial product that they have spent centuries perfecting. It's that knowledge that keeps them afloat.

COMMUNICATION
So why can't sales speak to production? Why can't production speak to suppliers? Why don't sales tell us what to make next year?
SOLUTION
Maybe we should get rid of divisions, lose purchasing, IT and HR, and start again with a clean sheet of paper and let people talk to each other.

THOUGHT – KNOWLEDGE

Where does the value lie in a company? The buildings? The stock? The good will?

A company is for sale for 100 million – a maker of a famous brand of chocolate. The buildings are worth 10 million, the stock 10 million, the brand 30 million, the goods and distribution 10 million. That makes 60 million. Something's missing. That fact is that even with all this lot, on day one we won't know how to do *it*. What is 'it'? Make the chocolate, wrap the chocolate, store it, stack it, buy the ingredients, wash the machines, fix the machines. So who does know? Not one single person, but everyone who works for the company. The 40 million is in the collective know-how of the whole workforce. Every employee you lose will lose you a bit of collective intelligence. Lose a forklift driver, and you lose the knowledge of how high you can stack Easter eggs before you damage them. But you do have the back-up of three other forklift drivers, who are hopefully clones of the first. But it is like losing brain cells; how many can you afford to lose? They say that drinking kills brain cells, but are they important ones? Maybe you just kill those insignificant childhood ones. Perhaps just the one that remembers your nodding wheely-duck toy. You don't remember your nodding wheely-duck toy? Perhaps you shouldn't have had that last gin and tonic.

When companies get into trouble they start laying off staff, but that is like saying that since the human being only uses one-third of its brain (that is a fact), then it would be sensible to save weight and conserve energy by having two-thirds of your brain removed. That is ludicrous, and you would cease to function. Maybe you would argue that you removed the wrong two-thirds, but I challenge you to remove any two-thirds and survive. In the company, just like the brain, the working knowledge lies in every cell and every employee. Think about this. Someone says your brain is performing at one-third of its capacity. The correct view would be to speculate that if you could get the rest to work, you would be three times more effective. This is what we need to do with people, they must all add value. Quite simply, if you pay them £100, and they generate £200, then you haven't got much to worry about.

LOOK FOR THE VALUE IN PEOPLE. KNOWLEDGE IS POWER. KNOWLEDGE IS VALUE.

THE SOLUTION?

Can you see the problem, or is it just me? It can't be. Some of you out there must be reading this and saying 'I know companies like that', or worse 'my company's like that', but when I suggest there may be a problem, people look at me as though I was mad. It is very frustrating for the jobbing guru to be told to come up with the latest cutting-edge idea. Worse, I suppose that the last cutting-edge ideas were a load of old bollocks, so into the bin goes Total Quality Management, Just in Time, Customer Care, Empowerment, Continuous Improvement, Excellence, Process Re-engineering. If you write about them, then you are rehashing all the same old things. If you mention them, then the client claims 'already doing it', or 'did that, didn't work'.

This lot had tried them all, and were currently deeply involved in 'benchmarking'.

'We know that we have slightly extended delivery times, and we have benchmarked our competitor and instead of 14 weeks, they offer 12 weeks delivery.'

'So they are crap too?' I interjected cheerfully.

Ignoring me, they continued. 'We recognise this to be best practice and have set up a work group to streamline our systems, and we are confident in the near future we can achieve a delivery time of, in most cases, 12 weeks.'

'Well, I tell you what,' I replied, 'Forget benchmarking, I will cut it down from fourteen weeks to three hours.'

A BLOKE WITH A WHEELBARROW

How? Lets get back to basics. All the preceding business theories mask some very simple truths. We make things or do things that people give us money for. It costs us money to make or do these things. If people give us more money than we spend, that is a profit. If they give us less, it is a loss. The people that give us money are called customers. They are hard and costly to find, so when we have found profit-making customers, we should keep them forever.

FINDING CUSTOMERS AND KEEPING THEM IS THE ONLY WAY TO GENERATE REVENUE. EVERYTHING ELSE WE DO INVOLVES US IN COST.

When we find a winning product or service, we will get more customers than we can handle, so we pay people to help us. They are called employees. At best, each one of these 'employees' should be a miniature replication of the business, and could generate profit that is way above their cost. We in turn should be able to trust them to do this. As we don't trust them for their ability, enthusiasm, intelligence, knowledge, loyalty or honesty, we have to install systems of supervision and counterchecking to prevent the mutinous dogs from ruining us. This accepted practice is the only thing that stands in the way of my solution. So that said, here is the solution that I gave to this company.

They would need a wheelbarrow, a mobile phone, laptop, and a single employee in the warehouse. The phone rings.

'Hello, thanks for ringing Acme, I'm Charlie, what can I do for you?'

'We want 35 × 47Ps.'

Charlie, looking around. 'Yep, I've got 'em, can I ask who's calling, please?'

'Brian Perkins.'

'And your company, Mr Perkins?'

'Chipolata Precision.'

Charlie lights up his laptop. 'Oh yes, I've got you. Hang on though, there is an outstanding account and you seem to be on stop. Do you have a credit card number that I can use?'

'Um yes, 344485567.'

'OK, got that. Well, I have settled the £748 owing and taken a further £438 for this order. That gives a total of £1286 and I am printing your invoice now. Thank you very much for your order, and I am taking the goods to dispatch as we speak.'

Charlie puts the goods in his wheelbarrow and takes them to the delivery truck. Well, less than the three hours.

Of course there is uproar at this suggestion. 'You can't do that! You are seriously suggesting that warehouse staff would be privy to sensitive accounts information!'

'And what's wrong with that?'

'Warehouse personnel can't be trusted.'

I know this is a recurring theme in this book, but why employ people you don't trust, or is it the case that we can't trust anyone and the human race is intrinsically untrustworthy? Or is it just the lower social orders that can't be trusted? In that case, it is a dreary hopeless old world and I think I'll go and lie on a beach somewhere while waiting for the four horsemen to come and give us all a jolly good clearout.

'Then who can be trusted to handle financial matters?'

'The accounts department.'

'OK then, give them a wheelbarrow and shove them in the warehouse.'

The reaction to that suggestion doesn't even need describing. I am sure you can guess it, but why not put accountants into the warehouse? Beneath their dignity? They don't have anything to do with customers? Waste of talent?

COD, CHIPS, PUDDING, COFFEE, AND TWO KNOBS

Now let's see what computers can do. Take my earlier suggestion that computers can often just be a way of transferring complicated and outmoded systems on to television. This is backed up by the massive variety of software and systems each department has to choose from. Accounts would use Bindweed Version 11.3, the drawing office would use Hair Trigger 5.6, of course all dedicated to specific tasks, but best of all an impenetrable mystery to any outsider. Networks were developed so that computer could speak to computer, but there were no worries as they all spoke different languages so there was no danger of the enemy (our colleagues) getting our precious information. People who protested were told that the systems were so diverse and complicated that it would be impossible to integrate them. There is an analogy here with the whole idea of process re-engineering. On a micro or macro or computing level, if you can make your bit complicated, mysterious and indecipherable, the reformers will leave you alone. There is however trouble brewing for these illuminati as there is modern software that can be dropped in like one of these ferocious lavatory cleaning bombs, and can literally cut through crap, leave everything sparkling and, in computer terms, integrate every element of the business.

This means that if you bust the knob off your washing machine and ring the manufacturer, then if the lady in the staff canteen picks up the phone, instead of wailing 'You're through to the wrong number,' she can say 'Who is calling please?'

She could then fire up her terminal, which also runs her till and normally does the mundane task of pricing cod, chips, and mushy peas. 'Ah yeah, we got you luvvy, you've got a Spin Freak 24! Bust the knob off it, heh? OK, I'll call up the service diagram. We got two knobs here, an inner and an outer. Both? OK, dispatch are putting them in a jiffy bag, and if you can pay me by credit card, you will receive it tomorrow morning. Thank you for your order.' Her takings that day are 400 cod and chips, 25 vegetarian meals, 65 yoghurts, 750 coffees. And two knobs.

Those senior management that I present this jolly scenario to shake their heads in horror and disbelief. The computers can do it, with training the people can do it if they want to, but the minds of the management just can't get around it. Let's encourage them.

KEEP THE CUSTOMERS AT BAY

There was a huge hoohaa about the Internet and how the world would buy everything over it. It sounded like the death knell for shops, travel agents, purchasing departments, sales and possibly all human life as we know it. I had my doubts. I am certain that without humans the whole thing is a non-starter. We will look at how a great Web site and people can work together to make an unbeatable sales team in a later section, but one thing did happen. People started to expect the speed that IT implied. They also expected the multiple access IT promised. If you look at the back of an old television, you will see that all its information is fed to it through a single aerial wire, and even when VCRs were invented, the signal had to cross through them first and then to the TV along this same single wire. Inside the TV there would be an electronic receptionist that would sort out the appropriate signal that was carried to the screen. That's all we knew, and we were happy. Look at the rear of a modern TV. It has Scart leads, they have dozens of pin and sockets giving immediate and direct access to every department of the TV, VCR, DVD, sound system and digital box. Now we expect cinema sound, interactive information and total control of all our viewing experiences in an instant. Companies can be the same with multiple access and communication. It is just that they don't want to because – here we go again – they don't trust their employees or worse, their customers. They want it all coming down that single wire where they can keep an eye on it. The idea of access beyond their control is terrifying, but then this makes them slow and useless.

A SHOCKING THOUGHT

The one thing that can be agreed about my case is that it certainly speeds things up. Is that important? Today's customers prefer speed to quality. Don't believe me? It is Sunday, you are doing some DIY. Visiting your local superstore, you ask for an Acme Diamond All Life Super Saw. 'They are on a three week back order. We have these in stock, the WanKee Cheepo Cut.'

Will you wait for the Acme? I think not. You won't wait three weeks, but let me frighten you even more. 'We are expecting some Acmes in, in about six hours.'

I still think you may not wait. A victory for the speedy but crap WanKee Saw Company.

WE MUST BECOME EASIER TO DO BUSINESS WITH.
WE MUST BECOME FASTER TO DO BUSINESS WITH.

THE PROJECT THAT WORKED

The Maxmonster Megalith Global Corporation, in its huge portfolio of chemical/pharmaceutical and additive companies, found that it owned 40 or so biscuit companies. In global terms, this was about 35 biscuit companies too many. One of their biggest and least efficient (third in size, 39th in efficiency) was in northern England. To slash and burn would have been politically sensitive, and it also had a good solid management team who would have been wasted on immediate closure. Its doom had to be subtly engineered. First, move the good personnel to other parts of the organisation, next put an idiot in command to guarantee a swift, but not too obviously swift, demise.

It is a strange phenomenon of management that the stupid rise to surprisingly lofty heights.

Someone phones you. 'Hi, can you recommend a person in your department for the fast track management programme?'

Of course you send your most valuable and productive team member. Most people however, me included, would use it as a great way to unload my idiot. Thus they get passed ever onward, ever upward. Of course, some are spotted and are culled, some destroy themselves, but like spores or sperm, nature produces thousands of them, and though brutally red in tooth and claw, only one needs to survive to become CEO.

The corporation located just the man they needed, well spoken, good family and a complete half-wit, but they had made one miscalculation, and that was that the stupid ones are sometimes so stupid that they don't know how to fail.

This chinless wonder surveyed his crumbling empire, and decided he ought to read a book on what to do. Fate dictated that he picked up books on process re-engineering. Gurus such as Hammer and Peters were his guide, and as the simple minded ones are wont to do, he started on page one and went by the book without question or deviation. Allegedly at some point in one of his books, Tom Peters makes the allegorical statement 'bulldoze your head office'. When I arrived at this company, huge yellow machines were clambering over an enormous pile of smouldering rubble, and our grinning hero was standing, hard hat at a jaunty angle and hands on hips, surveying this scene with some pride. Behind him, his management team arriving for work stood aghast at the destruction of their cosy habitat, but not for long because following the book, those that hadn't buggered off back home were soon dressed in boiler suits and were helping to dismantle a production line. Everyone was helping to clean, reset and reassemble the Crunchy Choc Crumble line. The book said it built team spirit. The book said once everyone from accountant to packer understood the mechanics of production, it would boost output, build quality control, and cut down-time. If Lucy, the chopped nut sticker, could identify a slack or poorly lubricated drive chain before it snapped, there would be great benefit, or even better, she could oil or adjust it. This little project however cost the company millions in down-time and lost production, whilst our dotty chum strode about saying 'no pain, no gain, speculate to accumulate'.

The powers that be gleefully saw these actions fulfilling their predictions of a swift demise and became positively ecstatic as middle management haemorrhaged away (he has read the chapter on empowerment).

TOO STUPID TO FAIL

It so happened that this huge biscuit works was in a particularly rundown neighbourhood and most of its menial recruits came from the area. One particularly slack-jawed, empty-eyed woman had for years shoved 144 Choco Dip Cookies into a box, taped it shut, and stacked them on a pallet. (Now our hero has read the chapter on talking to employees and making them into stakeholders.)

'Ah, Doreen, how, um, are you finding these, um, boxes?'

'They're a load of bollocks, beggin' your pardon, your mightiness.'

'Could you expand on that?'

'Well, they ain't always the same size, if they're small, they traps me fingers, if they're big, it busts the biscuits, 'cause they rattle about and I get a bollocking, and they sometimes splits. It's always the bottom ones and that ruins a whole pallet of biscuits.'

'Then you shall be in charge of purchasing the packaging. I shall have a phone installed here, and you can phone the packaging supplier yourself with complete authority.'

With that, he waved his magic wand and the sparkling dust of empowerment showered down upon the girls in packing, in true Disney fashion.

A couple of days later, a furious phone call was received from Sir Derek Findley-Parsons, chief executive of Panjandrum International Packaging. 'I say, I've just had some horrid, common woman called Doreen ring and threaten to cancel five million pounds worth of packaging if we didn't, quote, "get our sodding act together." Go and fire her now and let's have no more of it.'

'But she has got the power to cancel your order.'

'Then tell her not to be silly.'

'No, you tell her. She has the authority, not me.'

The next day, a fleet of Rolls Royces and Jaguars swept into the works and Sir Derek and his production director spent a very uncomfortable but productive day with Doreen. Millions in lost production and damage was saved on the spot, and soon the costly down-time was recovered by a massive increase in productivity.

As the managers left in droves it was seen that a clear overview of the whole process was held by the forklift drivers, who were given the position of company spokespeople. If you should visit this factory, you would be shown around by forklift drivers.

JUST COMMONSENSE

All this involvement also virtually wiped out absenteeism. The company moved up the rankings to second most productive and profitable plant. The workers have one simple ambition, TO BE NUMBER ONE.

The irony of all this is that it was achieved by simple minded naivety. I sometimes get viciously accused of espousing commonsense. 'We read Geoff Burch's book and at the end of the day, all his theories just boil down to commonsense.'

It is simple commonsense to:

- smile at every customer;
- start with 'Yes';
- be easy to do business with; and
- be quick to do business with.

The list could go on for pages, but they're just a few simple, commonsense ideas. Now go out into the High Street and try and buy, say, a laptop computer. You know that none of these simple things will happen. You know they should. The companies you are trying to do business with sort-of know they should. It just doesn't happen.

THIS BOOK, HOWEVER OBVIOUS, HOWEVER FACILE, MUST FIND OUT HOW TO MAKE IT HAPPEN FOR YOU.

Points to ponder

- The 21st century customer has been taught to expect speed.
- People will sometimes prefer speed to quality.
- If your despatch systems are based on a lack of trust, stop employing untrustworthy people.
- If your systems are set up to protect you from a lack of skills, then train.
- If you can't recall why your systems were set up, scrap them and start again.
- Do the wheelbarrow exercise and tell yourself why it wouldn't work for you. Then put your hand on your hip, toss back your tousled mane, laugh like Errol Flynn or Douglas Fairbanks, and declare, cutlass in hand, why it *would* work for you.

DISMAL WARNING

The only problem with this elegant and cheery idea is that management consultants have got hold of it. By charging massive fees, creating reports the size of encyclopaedias and putting in their killer robots, they have transmuted it into, on the one hand, an over-complicated load of nonsense, and on the other, a simple slash-and-burn policy. The pessimist says the glass is half empty, the optimist says it is half full, but management consultants say 'first take a smaller glass'!

ALL YOUR PEOPLE AND PLANT CAN ADD VALUE. YOU ONLY HAVE TO SHOW THEM HOW. DON'T CUT, MAKE THEM PERFORM!

CUSTOMER CARE ...
THAT OFFER'S FINISHED!

Oh, wasn't it all the rage? Customer care. Customer care seminars. Customer Care training. But, somehow it's lost its glitter, it's all a bit 20th century, 1990s. We have better, more modern, fish to fry. Anyway, it didn't work, but what didn't work, and what was it supposed to do anyway? Let me repeat the simple truth that I am sure you will find elsewhere in this book.

**FINDING AND KEEPING CUSTOMERS IS THE ONLY AC-
TIVITY THAT GENERATES REVENUE. EVERY OTHER AC-
TIVITY INVOLVES YOU IN COST.**

Let us now have a look at the second word, CARE. What does that mean? Do you have savings? Do you take care of them? What does that mean? It means you put them in a place where they cannot be nicked, and then you steadily try to add to them. Surely this must be the only definition of customer care. You lock your existing customers in with such levels of service that your competitors despair of ever stealing them away from you. Meanwhile, Sales, Marketing and, for that matter, EVERYONE ELSE, are quietly adding more customers, or that is the theory.

Let's imagine that you are the owner of a chain of motorway services, and inexplicably you wake up one morning, and you decide you need marketing. All the blue chip companies I ever work with tell me that they 'have marketing', but they always express it in the tone of voice that makes 'having marketing' sound like some kind of medical complaint, like piles or boils. Anyway, you wake up to find that without the correct ointment you have the dreaded affliction that is marketing.

People who offer marketing often have names like Gervaise or Tarquin, and they gambol and caper around their west London offices with sheer excitement at the prospect of 'marketing' your motorway restaurants.

'What you need,' pipes up Tarquin excitedly 'what you neeeeeed is a promotion.'

'Oh yes, a promotion!' choruses Gervaise.

Tarquin continues. 'What we'll 'ave is an autumn promotion, and the logo will be shaped like an autumn leaf to suggest to the customer that the prices are falling like autumn leaves.'

'Yes,' cries Gervaise, 'and every home in the country will receive an autumn leaf shaped voucher, and as long as the customer purchases one full-priced adult meal, they will receive a further adult meal entirely free.'

This is called a B.O.G.O.F. by the way – Buy one, get one free! But what exactly are these marketing people trying to achieve? Why did you hire them, and what was it you wanted them to do? When will you know if they have done it? Obviously you must set them objectives. To measure those objectives it would be good to have benchmarks and key performance indicators. Oh yeah? Down that route lies ruin, as Government has so cheerfully proved with its health and education policies. How, I will hope to prove to you a little later, but for now let's ask Tarquin and Gervaise what bang they are going to give us for our bucks.

They chorus in unison 'Footfall! Increased footfall.'

To translate for those of us who don't speak fluent marketing jargon, this means bums on seats, people coming through the door for the first time. What they don't do is increase profit, or increase sales (they are giving the food away, for Heaven's sake). No, they are simply increasing the number of people who give us a try. Is that what you wanted? So the answer is yes, you want lots more *potential* customers. The hard-faced salesmen of yore used to call them leads or prospects, and those we sold to or signed up would become conversions. The fewer that escaped, the better the conversion rate. A simple idea that has got lost in the mists of time and the obfuscation of new-think.

Consider this, have you ever eaten at a motorway service restaurant? Would you seriously want to go back? You would try to avoid eating there again, even if your life depended on it. Gervaise and Tarquin Marketing may have increased footfall, more customers pouring through the door finding out just how bad we are. Our offering is crap and we are spending good money to help people find that out, spending half of our turnover to piss off the population twice as fast as we used to. Perhaps someone should have explained to the 27-stone kid, with the badge that reads 'I'm Kevin, I'm here to help', and a little red boiler suit so tight it is flossing his bottom, exactly what promises the marketing company are making to our customers, and what we are trying to do. It is no good spending a fortune shovelling customers through the door if Kevin is shovelling them straight back out of it again.

THOUGHT

*What marketing and sometimes sales **really** do is create expectations. People always buy because they expect something. Does everyone who works with you know what that customer expects, and are they sufficiently equipped to deliver it?*

A JOLLY INTERLUDE

On visiting a major hotel, I noticed that the particularly vacant and preoccupied object behind the bar was wearing one of THOSE badges. 'I'M CAROL, AND IT'S EVERYWHERE I'LL GIVE CUSTOMER CARE.' She was diligently examining something that she had fished out of her left ear, gently rolling it between thumb and forefinger, before looking at it more closely. Finally becoming aware of me looking at her, she returned a challenging, gorgon stare. Trying to put her at her ease, I explained that I was simply taking a professional interest in her badge. 'Oh this,' she said, turning the badge towards her while still retaining a grip on her little treasure, 'that offer's finished! We bin taken over. That customer care thing was put on by the other lot, and they don't own us no more.'

I used to get mobs of pitchfork- and blazing-brand-wielding marketing people beating a path to my castle gates by suggesting that the whole marketing thing basically sucks, but that may not be true. After all, you can even get a degree in it, by jiminee. Lets examine then what marketing does, and doesn't, do.

I suppose at its simplest our enterprise is driven by our customer's inclination to buy the things that we offer. To make things that people want to buy, and to make them buy those things, we need to understand why people buy.

EVERYONE BUYS BECAUSE THEY EXPECT SOMETHING.

It's the customers' expectation of a problem solved, a certain level of performance, travel experience, or flavour – the list of what we expect could go on for ever, but test this for yourself. Whether you intend to buy a book of matches or a jet plane, pause before handing over the money and think about what you expect to happen.

I am not the first person to notice this, and loopy management consultants wasted no time in complicating this simple idea into a difficult and mostly barmy theory – one which, I must admit, I subscribed to for a while. When doing customer care consultancy, it was felt necessary to be able to define the difference between good service and bad service. I would look piercingly at my victims and say 'Do you ever give bad service?'

The penitent would nod sadly, the defiant would shake their heads violently, and the wearily undecided would shrug. Now the coupe de grass. 'How do you know when you are giving bad service?'

No reply, just the odd shuffle or embarrassed cough broke the silence. Then in my oiliest of oily voices: 'It is when we fall below our customers expectations. Good service exceeds customer expectations, bad service falls below customer expectations.' A gasp of recognition of this truth followed by rapturous applause. Every guru was spouting this and soon mission statements started to include 'to exceed our customers' expectations'.

A LITTLE TEST

Pounce on one of your employees, not a selected one but the first one you see (because that is exactly what the customer will do), and ask 'What do our customers expect?' They will not have the foggiest idea. So there is a huge barrier already.

A TRAINING IDEA

Go to everybody in your outfit, even yourself, and consider very carefully what it was that the customer expected. Whether you are a lawyer, taxi driver or ball bearing manufacturer, have a few minutes think about what your customer expected.

Now the trouble starts because although the preceding bits are worthwhile considering, it may not be a good measure of service.

A mad American friend of mine who runs a very successful service company, was listening to this tirade of mine and pulled me to one side. 'Geoff, have *you* ever had the misfortune to eat in a motorway service restaurant?'

'Well, yes.'

'As you drove in, what did you expect?'

'Horrid food.'

'Yep, and how much would you expect to pay for this horrid food?'

'Lots.'

'You expect horrid expensive food, and you want to use the customers' expectations as your benchmark for good service! Are you nuts?'

The poor old customer expects nothing good. They expect the worst: high prices, bad service. Try the hi-fi shop, the computer dealer – what do you expect? Confusion and ritual humiliation by sassy propeller heads.

Think about your own situation if the vacuum cleaner you just bought had bits missing. What would you expect at the discount electrical store, a fight? Dumb insolence? You book a last minute package holiday. Expectations – a night flight full of drunken yobs, horrid food, being bussed for hours to a place with cockroaches and a busy main road. Oh, these duplicitous suppliers, hoteliers, and retailers, but hold on a minute. This is our – the consumers – fault. We have said, 'Don't want to be sold to,' 'Price, not service,' 'Price, not quality.' Great staff cost money, finely made goods cost money, space on aircraft that fly at convenient times costs money. The joke is that the undemanding customer has entered into a conspiracy with the supplier that hides greed on both sides. It is called customer care.

AN INTERLUDE

I am being bullied once again – 'Be constructive, not destructive.' But as I am feeling dismal today, I think I will rub salt into the wound.

The customer strides in with a furious complaint that can only be satisfied by management. Instead of being greeted by 'Uh', 'Don't come in 'ere shouting at me,' or 'I can't do nothin' about this, you'll have to see me manager,' we are instead greeted by thoughtful, astute eye contact, and 'I am so very sorry you feel upset. I think the very best thing I can do for you is to bring this disappointing situation to my manager's attention.' The key phrase is 'the very best thing I can do for you'. Surely you can't disagree that this is a great way to get over the 'I'll 'ave to call my boss' conundrum? A great little tip to take away then, but now go into your local DIY superstore, supermarket checkout, wave down a white van, speak to a school child (tomorrow's employees), your own parts department. Do you really expect any of them to use that speech convincingly? Depressing, ain't it? Oh well, on, on.

Think about recruiting people with great attitudes. The last person you recruited was hired for their skill and then you fired them for their attitude. This time, look for someone cheerful, loyal and enthusiastic. You can then train them to do anything.

Let's take stock. People always buy because they expect something and from a customer care point of view, they don't expect much.

At the front end, where did they get these expectations from? One place is Gervaise and Tarquin. What marketing does is to create expectations, expectations that are strong enough to prompt the potential customer to give something a try. The problem is that marketing people can make their job easy by creating huge expectations and then leaving the rest to us, which has the potential for large amounts of trouble.

They can even win prizes for what I consider to be extremely dangerous campaigns. One I call to mind and you probably will too, is an advert for a hatchback car. The film opened on a parched desert, the sun beating down with suitable sun-beating-down music. As a lizard scurries under a rock to escape the searing heat (to suitable scurrying-under-a-rock music), a dust cloud approaches. In the dust cloud is a speeding hatchback car. In the hatchback car is a handsome man and a beautiful sleeping woman. Despite the rough terrain, silence reigns inside this ballistic vehicle except for an occasional but annoying squeak. The viewer is intrigued, teased into believing the worst. The car pulls into a mysterious old garage where a strange old man comes out with an oil can. He rocks the car and can hear the squeak. After carefully checking, everybody laughs to discover it's the beautiful woman's diamond earring squeaking. Gently he oils the offending earring and all is well. The car glides silently away into our expectations. Everybody agrees that it's a great advert. What does it get us to do? It gets us to buy the car. That is what the objective was, and that is the objective that was achieved. If you made cars, would you like more people to buy them? Yes? So Gervaise and Tarquin Marketing pocket their cash and bugger off. Job done. You see the advert and buy the car. The parcel shelf goes flumpety bump, the gear lever goes shish shish shish, and the speedo goes ticky tacky ticky. If you can hear an earring over that, or even the 40-watt stereo, you are a better person than I.

Off you go, then, to the marketing people? No you don't, you go off to some poor little sod who is sitting on an upturned bucket in Milton Keynes or somewhere, eating a cheese and chutney sandwich and you say to him ''Ere mush, I can't hear my wife's earring squeaking.'

'Do what?'

'You promised me that I could hear an earring squeaking.'

'I never did, I ain't seen you before in me life.'

What the poor little mechanic hasn't realised is that as long as the logo on his breast pocket is the same as the logo on the advert, he, in a global sense of the word, did make that promise and is responsible for keeping it, but lets repeat that question.

DO PEOPLE KNOW WHAT THE CUSTOMER EXPECTS?

Marketing and sales often have very simple ob- **THOUGHT**
jectives. For our restaurants they increased footfall, *Show your workforce*
for our cars, they increased sales. They did it by creat- *your adverts.*
ing expectations. The company then fails to deliver.

OBJECTIVES, AN INTERLUDE

I was going to describe the importance of objectives as one of the great business myths, but then that's not strictly true. I suppose setting objectives is useful, as are empowerment, benchmarking, and customer care training, it's just that the misuse and misunderstanding is very damaging. Firstly because it is damaging and secondly because people blithely believe they are doing good things, and that is even more damaging.

If you have ever met any loonies from training and development, I am sure you will have noticed their obsession with setting objectives. Mention a sales development programme, and they will want to set those objectives.

'We need a sales training course.'

'Yes, and what are your objectives?'

'We want the team to be able to sell.'

'Sell what?'

'Sell, um, to sell, er, to sell MORE! We want MORE!'

You want more? More what? Lets say for this exercise that you would like more money. The objective of this training module is to help you to get more money. Simple. If that is all you want, more money, the best person to train you would be a mugger. He could show you what alley to lurk around in, what sort of knife to carry and who to jump out on. If you have any doubts about the efficacy of this then, after a short period of instruction, you could get a sharp knife and go to the centre of any major city (you might have to queue up of course), and you could start mugging right away. You may think this a ludicrous concept, but it does achieve its objectives. Tell me, what can be wrong? We have reached the present goal of more funds! I hope your answer is consequences, consequences that are beyond that goal. You can see it, I can see it, everyone surely except muggers can see it. So, who trained that thing in the last car showroom you went into, the thing that leapt out from amongst the yucca plants and invited you to view its latest model? A mugger if ever I saw one.

Imagine the scene. It is the annual convention of finance managers and a keynote speaker is berating the crowd. 'What is the biggest problem facing finance today? Come on someone, tell us what is the biggest problem.'

An embarrassed silence, a cough, a shuffle, and then a cry from the back. 'Bad debt.'

'Yes! Bad debt. Do you know what the average debt recovery position is? 95 per cent, that means that 5 per cent of our revenue stream is completely lost to bad debt. OK, lets set an objective for the next financial year? Come on, lets be brave, what are we going to shoot for?'

'96 per cent?' calls back an uncertain voice from the gloom.

'No! No! Lets be brave, lets go for the big one double zero, 100 per cent. But how? How can we get 100 per cent debt recovery? Lets have a brainstorm. Anyone?' A hand rises. 'Terry, what's your idea?'

'I think that for any client that falls more than sixty days behind with payment, we should send them a venomous snake in a jiffy bag.'

'YES, that would shake 'em up. We could achieve our objectives with that.'

Some weeks later, you visit one of your favourite clients and you find him slumped in his chair, eyes staring sightlessly, two red puncture marks in his forehead, a ripped jiffy bag lying on his desk and something horrible slithering under the filing cabinet. All you can say is 'Sod it, the finance department got here before me'! They might have done, but why should they care? They achieved their particular objective.

It is a bit like when you are fitting a carpet and, to your horror, you discover you have nailed your budgie underneath it. The first solution that springs to mind is just to stamp it flat. It's no good, it just scuttles along and pops up somewhere else. The first cure for any problem is not always the best if you don't consider the collateral damage or unforeseen consequences that can arise as a result of that action.

If you were the captain of a galley and decided to incentivise the rowers by paying a bonus to those who rowed the hardest, the damn thing would go round in circles. Just like your enterprise, the whole team have to work in unison to reach a common destination. It helps to have a clear destination. It helps more if the whole crew know about it.

THOUGHT

To go back, sales or marketing are very rarely involved or care about delivery, which is stupid. They will increase pressure to achieve their goals, which causes even more problems for the deliverers. Plus the fact that its rare for the deliverers to be told what it is they are supposed to be delivering.

Objectives and incentives should not be departmental, but should be company-wide. We are all in the same boat.

Now allow me to show you how the spectre of 'customer care' arose from these difficulties. Firstly, it was believed that training modules should have some kind of scientific, quantifiable outcome. The problem is people, human beings, these strange hairless squashy things that eat and have problems. You may believe you are a person, that you employ people, that even your customers are people. Well that's no good, how can you have a successful enterprise when it depends on anything as unpredictable as people? Even Henry Ford is alleged to have said 'How come when I hire a pair of hands, I have to take a human being with them?' But not anymore. In this brave new world of ours there is this wonderful stuff called political correctness. We don't have to be bald anymore, just follically challenged; not short, altitude disadvantaged; the finance department are no longer the undead, just differently lived. Best of all, we don't have to employ people anymore. People can now be redefined as a re-source. You can manage a resource.

If you recall the early black and white Frankenstein movies, Professor Frankenstein was always portrayed as tall, aquiline, darkly handsome and of course completely barking mad, but he was always accompanied by this poor, twisted, hobbling thing. His faithful servant who would hobble off into the thunder-rent night to do his master's bidding, bringing back body parts for the terrible experiments.

'I've brought you a human leg, mathter.'

'Good, Igor.'

Now every chief executive has an Igor, and he's called the Human Resources Director. It is his job, amongst other things, to judge people's (sorry, resources') performance against goals, targets and objectives. This is combined with training initiatives, management programmes, and so on. He then has to report to El Supremo on this performance. The trick is that this performance must be expressed as a number and not one that relates to anything from the real world.

'Igor, how are they doing?'

'Very well, mathter.'

'Put a figure on that.'

'THEVEN.'

'That's good, is it?'

'Very good mathter, it was thix point two latht year.'

From this ludicrous buffooning comes the idea of key performance indicators, or KPIs. We now start to understand how individual (personal or departmental) goals are so important, and how the overall picture somehow fails to get associated with it.

Dodgy single dimensional graphs are created.

'How are sales going since we introduced the mugging module to the sales force?'

A steeply climbing graph is produced.

'Thales have shot up, mathter.'

'Good, good. And debt recovery since the venomous snake programme?'

Another encouraging graph.

'Nearly 100 per thent, mathter.'

'Good, is there anything else to concern us?'

Another steep graph is produced.

'Well, mathter, a lot of thtaff have been arrested.'

Another graph.

'Oh, there's been a big ryth in complainth.'

A declining graph.

'Oh, and a drop in repeat bith-neth and referrals.'

For the first time there may be just a touch of uncertainty.

'This is nothing to do with the mugging or venomous snakes, is it?'

'Oh no, mathter.'

So now they indulge in the modern commercial equivalent of casting the runes. A jolly little exercise called benchmarking. The idea is that you go off and look at your competitors' stupid graphs and compare them to your own stupid graphs. If the competitor is doing something you are not, you rip it off lock stock and barrel – no matter that it was a crap idea when they tried it. The result is that Igor returns with good news.

'Good newth, Mathter. I know what it ith that we're not doing that our competitors are.'

'Do tell.'

'They thay things, mathter. They thay things to the customers, mathter.'

'And have you made a note of theeth – erm, ah – these things?'

'Yeth, Mathter.'

'Well, teach them to our staff.'

This creates a madness called customer care training. Yes, it is a madness, because all you get now is a mugger that leaps out at you, holds a knife to your throat and says 'I'm Brian, your mugger for this evening. Thank you for sharing your wallet with me, have a nice day and missing you already.'

CONCLUSION
Glueing customer care words on to a vicious greedy uncaring company is a waste of time.

Lets disassemble this a piece at a time.

THE MUGGING

We can interpret this as over-pushy selling, complete contempt for the customer's ability to spot rotten goods or services, or over-enthusiastic marketing. If you have ever been mugged, then you know that soothing words to the victim will not put things right. Holiday reps go on customer care training courses. Bad, crowded flights, stinky food, cockroachy hotels and unarmed peasants, however well trained, cannot put that right.

Anyway, how can you train people in customer care? Personnel and training departments drivel on about uncovering training needs. OK, so if a Mexican terrorist leaps out at me, holds a gun to my head and says: 'Haya, Señor, I am Juan Almigon Perano, and I will shoot you in the head if you don't mend-a my-a television', I would be forced to say, 'But I don't know how to mend your television.'

'Hokay then, I will send you to college for six months, and you can learn how to mend-a my-a television'

Now he has uncovered a training need, but if he said 'I will shoot you in the head if you don't smile and be helpful and polite to me,' I would do so straightaway. I didn't need training to be friendly and helpful, I just needed a gun held to my head.

THOUGHT

If staff behave when a gun is held to their heads, what happens if you take the gun away? Yep, you got it, they go back to being crap. We have to change the culture so that being good is the natural state, then we won't have to spend our time chasing them.

A large DIY store rang me and said 'We want you to come and do one of your customer care training things for us.'

'Oh great! I'm glad I'm your first choice.'

'Actually you weren't our first choice.'

'No?'

'No, you were the eleventh! We have had ten very successful previous customer care training modules, haven't we, Igor?'

'Yeth, Mathter.'

'Module three was one of my favourites. We called that "Putting the Customer First", and we had a winning post and a chequered flag to suggest to the team that the customer was winning the race when it came to service.'

'Module five, Mathter.'

'Module five, magnificent! What we had then was a lion wearing a crown, which suggested to the team that the customer was king of the jungle when it came to service.'

'Theven, Mathter.'

'Ah, seven ....'

'Wait a minute,' I cried, 'If these modules were so successful, why have I got to try and train your staff?'

'Because they are still crap, Geoff!'

My first group were all the managers. Now remember that they had all been on ten previous customer care courses and they were becoming bored, if not actually mutinous. I greeted them, if not a little apologetically then as cheerfully as I could. 'I know you have all heard this ten times before, but when you meet a customer, for pity's sake, would you please smile?'

Immediately someone's hand shot up at the back.

'Yes?' I said pointing to a man wearing an expression so sour you would think he had been sucking lemons.

'Yes, I think you ought to know, before you waste too much of your time, and ours, you ought to know that we have DONE SMILING.'

But of course they have all done smiling. Go into any large retailer, factory or hotel, and the sour faced misery that greets you will definitely have 'done smiling'. They don't actually smile, but they have 'done smiling'. What a simple, facile, old hat, boring, we've already done that, spent millions on training, bit of advice that is: 'SMILE'.

CHALLENGE

Commonsense, boring, we've done that. Maybe so, but today, go and make sure everyone who works for you always smiles and acknowledges every customer (it's harder than you think).

OK, why smile, what have they got to smile about, what does it do for the customer, or profit, what's in it for them?

A STUPID CAT SHAKES HANDS

You can teach anyone or anything 'how', but it is useless if they don't know 'why'.

I have this cat. It has the intrinsic intelligence of a polystyrene ceiling tile, but by simply denying it food, I have been able to train it to shake hands with me. People watch with joy as the little chap holds out his paw.

'Oh look,' they cry gleefully, 'the pussycat is shaking hands with its master.'

Great, but what is it thinking? Is it thinking, 'Oh how do you do, master, I am so very sorry that I wasn't able to join you earlier, but I have just been having a poo in the garden'?

No, I tell you what it's thinking, it's thinking '————————'. Nothing! Absolutely nothing! Now its time for you to put this theory to the test. You may be amazed to learn that all of those big High Street names have spent millions on training their staff. All of them! For this experiment, you must stroll casually into one of these stores and loiter, whereupon it won't be long before you are pounced on. 'Can I 'elp you?' they cry. You, of course, are supposed to reply, 'No, thank you very much, I'm just looking.'

For this experiment, change the script and sow confusion beyond your wildest dreams.

'Can I 'elp you?'

'With what?'

Total panic! 'Pardon?'

'What do you want to help me with?'

'I don't know.'

'Then why did you ask me that, then?'

'I don't know why I said it – because they made me say it – I don't know why I'm saying it.'

At this point, your victim will break down and compassion dictates that you leave quietly.

CHALLENGE

Go back through your training programme and check that not only 'how' is taught, but also 'why'. If you can't see the 'why' don't even bother teaching 'how'.

There you have it, the customer care disaster. But why? The answer is quite simple and is probably very similar to the debacle that was process re-engineering. All the bits of your business have different concerns, even you. You want to spend less, earn more, and stop worrying, but customers are an obstacle to this cheery state of affairs. They are demanding, tricky and reluctant to part with their money. Life would be so much simpler without them but don't worry, your front line staff are at this moment doing their best to get rid of them for you!

Of course, the only fly in this ointment is as we have agreed before. The only thing that keeps us going is the customers' money.

LOSE CUSTOMERS, LOSE MONEY

On average, we lose 25 per cent of our customers each year. That is of course the national 'we'. You surely do better than that, but just think of the last 40 people you met in connection with your enterprise. Were all 40 regular customers? If it was only 30, is your business growing at 25 per cent a year, built on that solid unshakeable customer base? If not, where did the missing 25 per cent go? They went, brace yourself, because they were pissed off with you and your offering. Of course customers die, get captured by terrorists or leave to become Trappist monks, but in survey after survey, at least 90 per cent of lost customers are lost because they don't like your offering. Raised prices, unattractive designs, surly staff, an argument – take your pick, you did it. It's maybe something you had no control over, but you did it, consciously or not.

So what? Find new, fresh and unannoyed new customers. Live on the edge. Be a hunter, not a farmer.

ANOTHER SIDELINE

Actually not necessarily a bad thing. There are two ways of making money from sheep. You can leap on them, beat them to death, sell the meat, the bones and the skin. How many times can you skin a sheep? Of course, only once. But if you love the sheep, cuddle them, tend them when they are sick or depressed, you will build a relationship with them and finally the sheep will come to you and say, 'Baaaah! It ain't half hot in this fleece'.

In modern jargon we will use the relationship to become a problem solver. 'Have you ever considered being sheared?'

You can shear a sheep over and over again. In fact we can have a profitable relationship for life, but then sheep are such a pain in the arse, let's just eat the stupid things and have done with it. Who wants a life-long relationship with a sheep? This is the essential heart of successful high-pressure selling. You sell vacuum cleaners, double glazing, conservatories, life insurance, to sheep that you have no intention of ever seeing again, but rather more of selling later. For now lets assume that we would like to keep our customers.

Returning to our original formula, that finding and keeping customers is the key revenue stream.

Let's talk about finding. The two main ways at present are through sales, and marketing or word of mouth. I will dedicate a whole section to sales, so let's consider marketing once again. As a rule of thumb, it costs ten times as much to find a new customer as it does to hang on to an old one. You may have your own marketing division, but likely as not you use outside help in the shape of a PR or advertising agency. What is their stock in trade? Getting the gullible to give their trust and their money. That may be what they will do for you, but it is also what they did to you. Look at what they do another way. They communicate with complete strangers, people you don't know, people who don't know you, and they invite them to give you a try. You spend the whole of your budget on people you don't know and who don't know you. Imagine what would happen if you spent even a fraction of that on your current customers.

THE REAL CUSTOMER CARE

If we kept every customer forever, all new customers would simply grow our ever-expanding and profitable customer base.

They say customer satisfaction is the key. I say 'Oh Yeah?' I say 'I don't believe there is any connection between customer satisfaction and repeat business.' OK then, how do you know that your customers are satisfied? 'If they return,' you cry. 'Too late,' I call back – 'We haven't seen Mr Smith for a bit, he must be pissed off with us.' No, we must gauge satisfaction before the trouble starts. Then we must conduct a satisfaction survey. For this, we need the services of a woman with shoulders like an American footballer and wiry auburn hair that stands still while her head moves. She leaps out at people with a clipboard.

'Excuse me, could you spare me a few minutes of your time to …? Do you travel with any of the following …? Would you describe their staff as satisfactory or not satisfactory? Would you describe the reception you receive as satisfactory or not satisfactory? If you had a complaint, would you say the way it was dealt with was satisfactory or not satisfactory?' I won't bore you with the other fifty-odd questions because they are all very similar. It's the result we are interested in.

The result is a score, the outcome of a customer satisfaction survey. These surveys cost a fortune, serve no purpose, and always have the same answer. That answer is 94.6 per cent.

This book is causing me some truly serious worries, and this customer satisfaction thing is one of the most worrying. I read a very simple book on customer care by a very simple man, who simply said satisfaction surveys were a completely crap idea. If you read the high-falutin personnel and training magazines, books and learned papers, you would consider it an exact but complicated science. Can one ingenuous half-wit be right, and the massive people industry be wrong, I ask you? No, that's not a rhetorical question, I DO ask you. I ask everybody. At one seminar

I asked the whole audience 'Why do companies conduct satisfaction surveys?'

The most telling and chilling answer came from one person. 'To congratulate themselves.'

I got cornered once by a professor who actually 'professors' in this lunacy, and he bored the arse off me for hours with three-dimensional graphs and computer modelling of attitude swings. I could not comprehend most of the columns of computer figures, pie and bar charts that he wafted under my nose. I just gave a wry smile when, on the last page of thousands, I glimpsed the figure 94.6 per cent.

GRAB YOUR CUSTOMERS BY THE THROAT

Therefore, for my limited understanding, if not your's, let's take the simplest and most often experienced satisfaction survey. That is the thing that lopes up to you in a restaurant and says 'S'everything l'right with your meal?' to which you reply 'yes, thank you very much'. How did that start? Who was it that taught them to say that, and what is the plan if we say 'no'?

I have often been heard to say that if I owned a restaurant I would encourage my staff to grab the diner by the throat and drag their face close to theirs, saying 'Are you seriously telling me that this is the best meal you have ever eaten?'

But why am I asking them that?

My clients who own restaurants howl like stuck pigs when I suggest this. 'We know our food's rotten. Of course it won't be the best meal they've ever eaten, we can only hope it wasn't the worst. Why provoke the customer?'

We haven't got the time or space in this section to go into this too deeply, but the answer is supposed to be that if you can get the truth from the customer, however painful, it helps you to change. 'We need complaints,' I cry at meetings, 'welcome complaints'. Don't listen to me, that is just the oily ramblings of a smartarse business speaker wasting his breath for money. The truth is that these unpalatable truths should drive change, but none of the companies I have in mind have any intention of changing. Low wages, bad food, captive or desperate customers – that's their recipe, and they're sticking to it.

CRAP AND PROUD OF IT

I stopped at a motorway restaurant and had chicken and chips. The slack-jawed gibbon that served me could not have given a toss, the chips were soggy, the chicken had been turned to thin, greasy, chewy timber by the death ray lamp from the planet Zarg, and the price was a King's ransom. You have seen it, you have been there.

I met a friend who ran a mega-contract catering company, and I did my tirade. 'Are they mad? Do they have a death wish? Don't they care?'

Her reply stunned me. 'No,' she said.

'What do you mean, no? What about repeat business?' I rambled on at some length about skinning sheep.

'No, they don't care. They have millions of customers. If one doesn't return, there are a thousand to fill their place. Customers are stupid and if you can take another 40p per head by giving them rotten food, you soon become rich.'

'Well, I shan't be eating there again.'

'Yes, you will.'

Of course she was right. How many of you out there genuinely boycott motorway services, change banks or stop shopping from the huge electrical retailers where nothing works first time? I AM A CUSTOMER, I AM STUPID.

So what's in it for the shrewd business? There is a glimmer of hope. Us stupid customers don't change through inertia, we can't be bothered, but we are vulnerable to being enticed. A better, easier, nicer offer will have us away in droves. Imagine tasty, well

priced, home cooked food offered at the entrance of those services. I for one wouldn't walk past that offer. Of course our lazy, stupid competitors busily congratulating themselves with 94.6 per
cent won't see it coming. The slaughter will be bloody, and victory
glorious, but first we must build ...

... A CUSTOMER TRAP

Like all traps, the prey must find it easy to get into and very hard
to get out of. I suppose advertising and sales would be analogous
to bait, but I think that a tightly sealed box with lovely smells ema-
nating from it would be very silly trap indeed. We would crouch
watching in the undergrowth as a large beast sniffed and pawed
this large crate with a tasty morsel inside – and absolutely no way
to get at it. Eventually our quarry would tire and leave. The stupidest hunter reading this would see the flaw in this cunning plan,
so how come we lose our senses when it comes to business? We
bait our trap with tempting adverts and promises. We even pay
experts to identify exactly what prey we are after and help us to select the perfect bait. Millions have been spent developing exactly
the car that is meant for me. The advertising campaign was aimed
at me – dark, exciting, with a frisson of danger, big mileages with
a sporting edge. This is the one for me. At the showroom there is
no stock, but bored, smelly salespeople who put every obstacle
in my way. Well, Mr Carmaker, you can shove your car up your
bottom, I'm not coming back. The trick is to be easy to do business with and, as I have said elsewhere, the main spin off from
the high-tech economy is speed. Tempt me, then I want it now –
I won't wait. This is an important point which takes us back to
marketing.

Imagine deciding to put on a show and yet again employing
Gervaise and Tarquin Marketing. They decide to print the tickets
on gold foil and market them through commuter rail stations,
supported by TV and radio adverts. A cunning and novel plan,

because the shows will hub in commuter centres, an easy journey that the potential audience will know well. A success, the show is a sell out. We sit in the hushed and darkened auditorium. As the curtains part, we are faced with a badly-lit stage, some half-empty boxes and a few bored kids milling about. Is this a new undiscovered Beckett, or have we forgotten something? How about the show? Great ticket. No show, and a load of skinned sheep. Your only salvation is to bugger off with the money before they catch you. If that is not your strategy, the show must be better than the tickets promise. Make it the best show in the world and the audience will find you.

WORK ON THE SHOW, NOT THE TICKETS

Our trap must be open for our prey to wander into, unhindered, happy and without suspicion. We must become easy to do business with. I was waiting at a car hire company to collect a car and was listening to their receptionist. She was friendly, polite, better than most even, but her favourite word was 'NO'.

'Hello, my company has booked me a car but I can't remember which company it was with. Is it you?' 'Name?' 'Jenkins.' 'Company?' 'Higgins Precision.' 'Let me check.' A while later: 'No.'

Turning to me she said 'I get dozens of them every day.'

Dozens, let's say ten. What if she had said 'I can't find it right now, but I have got exactly the car you want and we would be very pleased to have you as a client'? That would bring in about £600 per day, or around £150,000 a year. Doesn't that sound good? Why doesn't every car hire firm, builders' merchant, bolt stocking company or anything you care to ring, tell their people to stop saying 'no', and turn every call into business? Now depress yourself. Go into, say, a builders merchant, look at the vacant-eyed thing with the stub of pencil behind his ear, and imagine him saying anything positive or business building. This is going to be an uphill battle, but one we are going to win together because there is everything to play for. First step, try and do business with your own enterprise. Was it completely obstacle-free and easy? Did you fall into your own trap?

ONE NOTCH ABOVE CRAP

OK, lets get back to our customer satisfaction survey. We want them in, and we want them to stay in. In other words, we want repeat business, to keep them coming back for life, but as I said, I don't feel there is a connection between satisfaction and repeat business. If you object to this theory, think about it. When did you last say: 'ere, you ought to try that new restaurant in the town. We went there the other night and it was ... satisfactory'?

Make no mistake, satisfactory is one notch above crap! Look at your microwave oven. It's OK, isn't it? You brought it home from that superstore in its cardboard box, you puzzled out 30 per cent of the instructions (enough to warm through a frozen lasagne) and there you have it. Did that store win you as a customer for life? Will you always buy the same make of domestic appliance? Satisfactory? Sure, but it isn't enough. If I asked you where you bought it, you might tell me. If I asked you what you thought of it or the retailer where you got it, you might say 'OK'. That is satisfactory.

Let's then take stock of the satisfied customer. They don't have any particular reason not to do business with us again, they don't feel it is necessary to tell people about us, they don't suggest that people give us a try. As this is the benchmark that the faceless hotel chains, airlines and mass manufacturers set as their goal, a great myth has grown around the satisfied customer. Because this is the best the multinationals can attain, their tame gurus spout rubbish like 'satisfy a customer and they tell no one, upset one and they will tell 20 people'. Therefore if you satisfy 95 customers, the upset five will create 100 enemies, so even at 95 per cent (near enough to 94.6 per cent to make little difference) we are battling to stay ahead of the game. What a load of old cobblers. This is followed by 'customers only stay loyal till they find a better offer'. I suppose that bit's true, but it is stated in a tone which implies that customers are mindless, disloyal chancers whose ingratitude is only matched by their greed. The best we can hope for is to satisfy them. Again, a great opportunity, because if that's what our competitors believe then their customer base will be totally vulnerable to our advances.

Let's go over the border of satisfactory, and visit the dark and cheerless land of crap service and the frightening territory beyond. It would be reasonable to assume that most service is crap, it's just that we tolerate sour faces, poor product knowledge and total lack of interest. If surveyed, we describe that as 'satisfactory'.

In a recent survey, a high percentage of staff admitted (in confidence) that far from being just bored or disinterested, they were actually INTENTIONALLY rude! We suffer that; they resist our refund request, cock up our order. We would rather not go back. We don't bother to talk about it much, but should they really wind us up, cause us some anguish or loss, then not only do we avoid going back, but we start telling loads of people. If it gets to litigation – or worse, TV consumer shows – we tell the world. A dazzling little turd then starts to bob in the corporate swimming pool: the reverse recommendation.

'Where can I book a holiday?'

'Anywhere except Visigoth Travel. They are truly awful.'

The glittering goal our competitors are after is 'doesn't really matter where, they're all as bad as each other'.

DELIGHTED CUSTOMERS SUCK

But we can do better than that, can't we? Do it right and the world's your lobster.

I bet you've guessed where we are going now. You think I am going to talk about 'delighting the customers'. I'm not. I think that is a really stupid idea as well. For the very few of you that have not come across this, let me explain. Some prat sort of realised that there was a slight whiff of rotting fish about this satisfied customer thing, so they asked themselves what was better than satisfied. EUREKA! DELIGHTED! From this came the philosophers' stone of personnel and training, the alchemy of HR, turning dross into gold. We had delighted customers coming out of our ears. Some cunning companies even used the jolly ploy of dashing a line through the part of their mission statement that said 'satisfied' and scrawling 'delighted' in its place. What a joke. What a wheeze. How gritty, how streetwise, how 21st century. What complete bollocks. When you went to collect that hire tool and the greasy chimp covered your car in oily finger prints and dents, were you delighted? You should have been, they put it on your leaflet, they painted it on the wall, they have even embroidered it on the chimp's boiler suit.

A JOLLY WHEEZE

If a company screws you about, torture them by reminding some senior director of the wording of his mission statement. Tell them it is a promise you expect to be kept: 'but I am not delighted. What are you going to do about it?'

That's just me being bitter and twisted, but be fair, when have you ever been delighted? A surprise birthday party, a Rolex from a happy client, or your first really really powerful motorcycle; 'delighted' is a really dodgy benchmark. Tom Peters came up with WOW or the WOW factor, the idea being that you do things that make the customer say 'Wow'. I like old Tom, BUT take one of his suggestions – your accountant sends you a set of competently and accurately produced figures. You pull them from the envelope, they are what you expect, you are satisfied. 'WOW' suggests the accountant add something that makes us say 'WOW'.

'Wow, look, he has included next year's business plan.'

'Wow, an amusing shaped vegetable.'

'Wow, a live vampire bat.'

'Wow' and 'delighted' really cannot be sustained. It's like rushing up to people and shouting 'Boo!' You may surprise them once or twice, but if oft repeated is likely to get you a punch in the face. And anyway up, just look at the staff in these 'delighted' and 'wow' establishments – you have got to be joking. We customers may be a bit stupid, but I am not so gullible to say 'Wow' or be delighted with greasy chips, cheap clothes or cheerless hotel rooms just because the idiot's badge tells me to.

So just lets think about this satisfied customer thing for a moment. As we have seen, a satisfied customer takes our service quotient just a fraction over the line called 'crap'. Just below it are customers whose technical description would be 'couldn't give a toss'. 'Satisfied' and 'couldn't give a toss' perform in very similar ways. Lets do the test.

> *Question: Do they tell anyone about us?*
> *Answer: No, not unless they are asked.*
> *Question: Do they send anyone to us?*
> *Answer: Nope.*
> *Question: Do they use us again?*
> *Answer: If it isn't easier to use someone else.*

Continue below the line until you have provoked the customers beyond all reason. They can now be defined as Barking Furious.

> *Question: Do they tell anyone?*
> *Answer: Boy, oh boy, do they!*
> *Question: Do they send people to us?*

Answer: Their lawyers.
Question:. Would they use us again?
Answer: Flying pigs?

This is where the lunacy about cross customers telling everyone and satisfied customers telling no one comes from, but as we have seen, satisfied is only a step above crap.

I had a teacher who hated me but could never pin anything on me, so on my reports the old git would write just one word: 'ADEQUATE'. Damned by faint praise. 'Delighted' doesn't hold water. Let's look at 'loyal' customers. They tell everyone, they send anyone they can, and they would walk through blizzards, across deserts and burning coals to come and do business with us.

Instead of Marketing spending a fortune trying to persuade complete strangers to do business with us, perhaps we should spend time and money on the loyal customers. Imagine if all your current customers brought a new customer in. 100 per cent increase in business. I would like to see Marketing top that. Businesses just can't see this and hammer away at ever more exotic and less successful campaigns.

The corporate powers find this lack of success frustrating and cannot understand why neither their staff nor the customer will play ball. To this end, they decide that this should become a mission. Time for the halfwits in marketing to create my all time favourite.

THE MISSION STATEMENT

I am often hired to secret shop various organisations and on one occasion I was invited to produce a report on theme parks. Starting in the UK, myself, my wife, and two borrowed children (my own being too large and unruly) visited a large theme park. The woman at the pay desk ignored us completely, taking our money and impatiently moving us through without even looking up. Eye contact is a vital part of this, but how do you get the bored part-timer/student/escaped lunatic to do it? We will have to cover the 'how to' stuff in a moment, but for now suffice it to say this was not a great start to my leisure experience, plus the fact that it was tipping with rain. As we trudged around this place with our shoes squelching, I was really feeling dismal. It was at this nadir I encountered *it*. By 'it' I mean the mission statement. Painted in huge bold letters for all the visitors to read. WELCOME TO THE LAND OF HAPPINESS AND ENJOYMENT, WHERE ALL YOUR DREAMS COME TRUE. Who are they trying to kid? Why put it for me to read? They should put it for all their staff to read. Mission statements are the bane of my life. They are usually so contrived: 'THROUGH CUSTOMER FOCUS, DEDICATION TO SERVICE EXCELLENCE AND INVESTMENT IN PEOPLE, OUR GREATEST ASSET, WE AIM TO BE WORLD CLASS LEADER IN THE GLOBAL LAVATORY BLEACH INDUSTRY.' Oh, come on. Before we continue, go to everybody who works for you (employed or as a supplier) and ask them to quote your mission statement to you. None of them will know it (if one crawly lickspittle does ingratiate themselves by knowing it, then ask them to explain what it means). If that is your mission, it means it is your destination, your target. If you own a bus or haulage company, imagine the horror of asking a driver if he knew where he was going and having him reply 'no', but all the people who work for us have no idea where they are going.

The fun really starts when your staff start to impact on your customer, usually in complete contradiction to the mission statement. I remember bearding a knuckle bumper about something I wasn't happy about. I pointed to the mission statement. 'Look, mush,' I said, 'I am most certainly not –' pointing my finger at the offending word to underline my ire, ' – delighted'.

His reply, 'D'you what?'

'Delighted, I am not delighted, in fact I am stinking, howling, sodding furious.'

Quite simply, no one had ever explained that this was what they wanted from him. If they had, they would have realised that he could never deliver 'delight' to anyone.

SWIVEL ON THAT!

Imagine driving down a country road when a large lorry pulls across in front of you. Cheerily you toot toot your horn to let him know you're there. Immediately a huge hairy hand shoots out of the window, a single digit is thrust skywards, accompanied by 'Swivel on that!' As the truck lines up in front of you, this statement is revealed: 'Happyvale Bakery, baking bread because we love you.' Who thought that up? The impact that driver had on us was far greater than any mission statement. Bury all your crawly, bum-licking advisors in a shallow grave and get back to basics.

When I was a kid, there were times when I was so stressed that I couldn't sleep. You may think that is a terrible thing for a child to suffer, but it was great and it was called Christmas Eve. So dribblingly, jimping, jumping, bouncingly excited that I couldn't sleep. The night before you decided to make meat pies, or ball bearings, or be an accountant, or the night before you started this job, you knew how good you could be – the yummiest pies in the world, the roundest ball bearings, the cleverest accounts, you could turn the company around. You knew that so well you could taste it. You were so excited about that passion, you wouldn't have slept that night. Now you know how good you can be. Customers' expectations? We know the poor old customers expect nothing, but you know just how good you can be. THAT'S YOUR PASSION. THAT'S YOUR MISSION. To make everyone who touches you infected with the hype of knowing just how good you can be. When the people who work with you (even if they're family) understand that passion clearly, they have two simple choices. They can be AMBASSADORS OR ASSASSINS.

THE DISMAY BUT

A lot has been said about Disney and one also has to be a little careful what one says because, like most American organisations, I should imagine they are quite litigious – so, carefully, I will say that they do seem to make it work in the Magic Kingdom. Everyone has heard of the CEO that picks up litter, and hundreds of other great customer service stories. You do get what you expect at Disney …

You are waiting for the 'but', aren't you? Well, of course I have got one. Let's just see what is good first. The real key is that they have taken their core passion and got everybody to deliver it 100 per cent of the time. I know I'm now going to shatter a lot of dreams right now, but you need to know this. Inside Mickey, Donald and Goofy are people. I know that's a shocker, but here's the point. You will never see Mickey lounging with his head hinged back, smoking a fag – unlike the Little Red Riding Hood I saw at a UK theme park, head unscrewed and enjoying a hand rolled ciggy while leaning against the enchanted cottage. An assassin if ever I saw one. How can Disney, using the same part-time, student raw material do it, and we can't? Because they take it very, very seriously indeed. It is a dictatorship of their values and to them that is the most important thing. Not realising that this is the key, people try to import or export the Disney thing. Even Disney themselves – is EuroDisney a success? Can you make French people friendly? I couldn't possibly comment, but when a major bank sent its senior managers to learn the Disney way, I really had to doubt their wisdom. What on earth were they expecting to learn? The only thing that I saw they brought back was the idea to paint a line on the wall in every branch with a sign that reads 'If you don't come up to this line, we can't serve you.'

They miss the point. What we need are people who are ambassadors of our beliefs. You would hate to go into a funeral director's and find the staff in Mickey Mouse outfits. Say, however, you were in charge of the Spanish Inquisition and recruitment and motivation had to be based on your passions. The idea is to terrify and torture people until they admit to being heretics, then you burn them at the stake to scare the shits out of everyone else. Donald Duck is no use to you here. Staff with red cloaks, studded leather, red hot pokers, and the simple joy that just comes from hurting people, vicious and uncompromising – they are great ambassadors. It's the sensitive, forgiving ones you want to weed out, because they are assassins. No one confesses to an inquisitor who apologises and isn't afraid to cry! Think again, what was so exciting about your thing that it kept you awake that night, the sizzle of hot tongs on frightened toes, the hum of accurate lathes, the aroma of beautifully cooked food or the excitement of a perfect audit? Get it, taste it, bottle it and sell it hard to everyone who works with or for you. Tolerate no mutiny when it comes to delivering your passion.

'HO HO HO,' SAYS BONGO THE BEAR

As we continued to shop this particular theme park, my depression grew. The pay kiosk, the mission statement, the rain. We trudged on miserably. Then, to my surprise, out from a bush leapt an eight foot tall, purple, furry bear! This thing was holding a bundle of gas-filled balloons. 'Ho, ho, ho!' it cried, 'I'm Bongo the Bear, what's your name?'

As this apparition towered over me, I managed to stammer out 'My name's Geoff.'

The bear returned 'Not you, dickhead, the kid.'

Oh how we laughed, actually Bongo the Bear had cheered me a little, so when the kids started badgering for a go on the roller coaster, I acquiesced with very little fight. We arrived at a sign that read 'This queue is two hours long.' Their logistics were excellent, because an hour later we were by a sign which said 'This queue is one hour long'. Accurate operations department then. Visualise the scene, one hour's worth of wet miserable people in front of us, one hour's worth of wet miserable people behind, and all of us trapped in a sort of modified abattoir cattle crush sort of thing. We were all standing patiently, dripping, squelching and shuffling forward one step at a time. Then panic broke. Panic with nowhere to go, people tried to climb the barriers or the trees. Women screamed, children cried, but what was the cause? Then we heard it in the distance, faintly at first, but coming nearer: 'Beep, beep, bugger off!' What on earth was coming, ever onwards? 'Beep, beep, bugger off!' Then the crowd parted like the Red Sea, and all was revealed. There was a horrid, scabby old man on an electric trolley thing with whirling brushes on the front and as people got in his way, he would hit the horn and shout 'Beep, beep, bugger off.' We could still hear him as he vanished into the distance. I wrote the report on these parks and there was uproar. Beep Beep's management were particularly upset and felt I had been unfairly harsh. So I agreed to meet them. 'Who was the Beep Beep guy?' I asked.

'Oh, that was Charlie the sweeper-up, that was.'

'I guessed that, but where did you find him?'

'Advertised, wanted sweeper-up, must be good time keeper.'

'It doesn't mention happiness or enchantment.'

'Well it wouldn't, that's Bongo the Bear's job ... didn't you meet Bongo the Bear?'

'Yes, but ...'

'Oh, I think we see what's worrying you – Charlie is on a bonus.'

'Great! How's that calculated?'

'Circuits of the park!'

Circuits of the park – he goes round like Michael Schumacher on that thing.

It may not come as a surprise to you that this is one of my favourite stories, but nothing is as simple as it seems. At seminars I tend to act out this story and then I pounce on the audience.

'Ok, then, your mad Uncle Harry dies and leaves you this theme park! Whoopee, you cry, and off you go to visit it. To your horror, you see Beep Beep. Now you employ him, what will you do with him?'

The first person I leap on cries out with a knee-jerk reaction 'sack him'.

'Oh sack him, that's nice, that is.'

The next person avoids that trap and says 'train him'. Train him to do what? 'What?' is the first big problem. The shouting and abuse, perhaps. So a bit of gentle counselling soon gets Charlie gliding silently around the park. I arrive to secret shop again, with a trusting child holding my hand.

'I like it here, it's so nithe and quiet,' the moppet lisps. We hear a gentle rustling whisper, a hum, and subdued whirring. A swish, a swish, and it's gone, as gently as it came. I glance down and to my horror all I can see is a shoe and an ice cream.

' 'ERE, STOP, YOU'VE 'OOVERED UP ONE OF ME KIDS!'

'Don't worry, Sir, when we empty the bag at the end of the day, any little boys and girls we find will be returned.'

What Charlie had done with the beeping and shouting was to develop on the face of it an illegal work practice that allowed him to do his job safely. To wit, clean the park without mowing down the visitors. He can't be blamed. We can, we employed him, but I think we gave him the wrong job.

YOU MIGHT BE READING THE WRONG BOOK

Perhaps we should cross a bridge here. What do you think you are reading? Is it a light airport read, or a business direction landmark that will be discussed long and hard at management schools? Apparently I am a business guru. I used to trundle about as a cheery idiot but because of my presentations or books, someone referred to me as a guru. Everything is different when you are a guru, and I felt I should examine the work of other gurus. My word, some of them write complicated stuff with complicated formulas, three-dimensional graphs and in-depth studies of very complicated reports. If you work for a multinational, there is sure to be some of this stuff knocking about in your company. Might I suggest that none of it works dramatically or even at all? Dare I suggest that money spent on these huge consultancy packages is almost completely wasted? At the other end of the scale, there are all sorts of chancers strutting their stuff on the circuit or around the book stalls – you name it, change, body language, customers, or sales. They offer it all. Strangely enough I have often found their simple advice the most useful. 'Smile', 'Don't take no for an answer', 'It's the customers who pay our wages.'

A true academic asked me if I knew why his mighty tome wasn't selling. By the kilo, his book would have been the bargain of the year. I struggled through it and hated every bit. It bored me to death, it confused me and I understood little, but hidden in there was a nugget, a real gem. In its simplest form, it is a winner. I may have nicked it, it may be in this book, but the point is let's get the simple stuff working first. If finding and keeping customers *is* the only way to generate money, then simply Charlie is pissing them off. He hasn't been told not to, and even if he was, we told him that sweeping was his prime directive. We punish or reward on his effectiveness as a sweeper. Very simply, we need Charlie to understand what the overall passion is. If that explanation has come from an international management consultancy, then Charlie won't understand it. Of course he understands 'smile', 'have a nice day', but he doesn't understand *why*. I hope this book isn't too simple for you, but we must achieve the simple things first. As I want this book to be a massive best-seller in the States, I am probably shooting myself in the foot by suggesting that occasionally not all Americans are necessarily the sharpest knives in the box, but maybe that simple single-celled dedication to the perfect burger, that great hair-gel experience, aquatic family fun, or whatever, is the secret of their success.

You own a theme park. A theme park is a form of entertainment. If Charlie is there, then he must first and foremost be part of the entertainment. Put him in a Bongo the Bear suit, and use his experience. He proved that when he was noisy he was safe. Then make it entertaining noisy. Make his sweeping machine look like an old fashioned locomotive with a loud steam whistle. 'Whoo, whoo! Coming through, Bongo the Bear cleanin' up the park!'

CUSTOMERS, WHO NEEDS 'EM?

This customer care thing has been about for yonks and yet I see no sign of it at all. Being on the seminar circuit means that I haunt the faceless hotels that are the only ones large enough to accommodate a conference of 500 to 1000 people. The price they charge is astronomical. You may be reading this book 40 years from now, so believe me I think that £200 per delegate per 24 hours is a lot. A thousand people times £200 times three days – that is £600,000 worth of business. Forget the surveys of the woman with the shoulder pads; I ask the delegates face to face 'Would you come back here next year?' Answer: 'No, not if we can help it.'

Where do we start, tepid cheap coffee, joke food at the Gala Dinner (fishy chicken and frozen veg), and surly stupid staff? Six hundred thousand pounds walking away. Are they nuts? No they are not nuts, but they are stupid. As the feeding frenzy of IT, telecoms and dot coms grew unabated, Willy Winkle Dot Com, D-Igalot Systems, and Chipalot Technology all had money and people coming out of their ears. Conference after conference, you couldn't find space at any venue, but think about this every time the phone rings in your thousand-room hotel and you hear the staff saying 'No, those dates are not available.' That is money walking away. I hear the whistling of a chill wind as the tumbleweed blows along the deserted streets of the M4 corridor, a fragment of newspaper with the headline 'more technology stock in crash misery' catches for a moment against an abandoned Porsche. Where is the feeding frenzy now? What if your people had always said, 'Yes, it would be our pleasure and delight to accommodate your conference. As this is our busiest time, we may have to use one of our partner hotels, but we can handle it all from here'? And so, when the final surviving company book that final farewell conference before we switch off the lights, you get to host it while your competitors have long since become smoking ruins or hostels for illegal emigrants struggling to leave. THAT IS WHY WE DO CUSTOMER CARE. THAT IS WHY WE DO SMILING. TO SURVIVE.

Smiling, welcoming, acknowledging every precious, valuable, money-spending customer. Back at our theme park, that thing at the gate. It has got to smile or it has to go. Was that difficult? So why doesn't every high street shop, burger bar, or hotel say that? Staff training, just say 'SMILE. BE ATTENTIVE AND POLITE OR SLING YOUR HOOK'. End of training.

THEY ARE THE BEST YOU ARE GOING TO GET

I do have a slightly gentler way. It's based on a strange idea that I have once in a while and it may not be true, but during my gentler phases of the moon I could be convinced that no one actually does a bad job on purpose. You are probably recoiling in surprise at this, but think for a moment. Even the most mutinous, dishonest or lazy member of staff cannot stride home with a spring in their step, shut the front door of their home behind them and sigh with ecstatic joy 'What a fabulous day at work, I did a truly crap job!' If that seems unlikely, then the unbelievable conclusion must be that they would be happy doing a good job. Lets not beat about the bush. Fact: kids come out of school useless, with no manners, aggressively stupid, and yet completely intimidated by normal human contact. Nil desperandum, that is our raw material and we must do the schools' job and attempt to turn them into useful functioning human beings.

What is partly our fault is that in the same vein as Charlie, we give them jobs to do – shelf filler, floor sweeper, lawyer or surgeon. No, I haven't lost my mind, the last two apply. That thing in your local supermarket with the bright blue sticky plaster covering his, or her, 'all coppers are bastards' tattoo is probably a medical student earning part-time money. All rights and no responsibilities. That trainee at the law practice may have a first in Tort and Easements, but does he know that casual enquiries on the phone are potential clients, and that by politeness and asking questions they can be secured and will pay his wages for a long time to come? If he doesn't know that it is your fault not his but then, on the other hand, perhaps you keep them too busy to help secure new business. But how busy, busy with more important things?

TOUGH TRUTH

If people are disloyal or don't help to win customers, no matter how clever they are, they are assassins and you should get rid of them.

DON'T BOTHER LOCKING UP AT NIGHT

Sometimes my job is to be a motivational speaker and employees are herded in to hear my words of wisdom. I dance and gambol, entertaining, cajoling, putting the message across, and sometimes they are amused and entertained. I suppose even listening to me is better than working. Did I do a good job? I ring the next day. 'Oh yes, I think they enjoyed what you said,' I am told. 'They've all gone off smiling at customers – a bit scary actually,' but if I were to ring the next year, they wouldn't even remember who the hell I was.

Say I was a security consultant and said to my rapt audience 'I have an idea that will help security' – pause for effect – 'Try locking up at night.' A gasp of surprise and recognition. I phone the next day. 'What a great presentation, we've all been buzzing. Everyone took turns in locking up, and do you know, virtually nothing got nicked last night.' Ring in a year. 'How is it going?' 'Not too well, actually. A lot of stuff is getting nicked.' 'You are still locking up?' 'Well … not as much as we used to. Marion always enjoyed the locking up, but she left to have a baby.' Of course that is absurd, but I would rather have stock nicked than lose customers. Hanging on to those customers is MORE important than security.

SIGN IN A NEW YORK DEPARTMENT STORE CHANGING ROOM:

> *'Please feel free to take in as many garments as you would like to. If you want more, call and our staff will bring them.'*

I would rather shop there than at the 'only two items allowed per person into the changing room' shop. They assume my dishonesty.

I ring a year later. 'Are you still being nice and welcoming to the customers?'

'Well, not as much as we used to be. As soon as the staff started being nice to customers, we got really busy, so we are too busy to be nice to all of them, but we are still quiet on Tuesday afternoons, so we have a "lets be nice to the customers" hour.'

'Every single customer must be acknowledged.'

'We're too busy.'

THE KID HAS HAD HIS HEAD RIPPED OFF

These poor gormless kids have one tenuous thread remaining that may connect them to the real world, and that is their Mums. In their simple way they can communicate with their Mums. As you will see in the sales section, they could sell to their Mums. They most certainly would always say 'hello' to their Mums.

How busy have you got to be before you would fail to say hello to your Mum?

Your company is a busy DIY superstore, and in the centre of the store is a huge display of ornamental paving slabs, built into a giant pyramid surmounted by a stone pissing-cherub fountain. It is a busy bank holiday and the place is packed, seething with people. They're all there, the family with the pit bull and shell suits – and their child, bouncing, jumping, and with a crusty trail of snot from its nostrils, decides to climb the aforementioned pyramid. Too late your supervisor notices the little chap aboard the cherub, merrily rocking to and fro. 'Stop tha – ' It's too late, child and statue plunge to the ground. Child hits first, statue crashes on top. With a sickening thud, the child's head is ripped off; the mother is hysterical: 'Me baby's 'ad 'is 'ead ripped orf!' Shocked customers are rushing about screaming as the headless torso flaps about in Heavy Gardening.

Your supervisor approaches and whispers in your ear, ' 'Ere, there's some kid 'ad 'is 'ead ripped off in Heavy Gardening. Get a shovel and clear it up, it's upsetting the customers.' So off you go, and scoop up this head. Now consider the situation. A packed, hysterical store, and you with a human head on a shovel. How much more busy do you want to be? How much more busy could you possibly be? Then in comes your mother. You've never been busier, but do you walk past your Mum with a head on a shovel and not say a word? Of course you wouldn't, you would probably say something like, 'Oh, hello Mum, can't stop just now, some kid got his head ripped off and I'm off to the skip with it but hang on, I'll be back in a minute.' See, Mum acknowledged and task completed. Just imagine every customer is your Mum.

Actually if you can get everybody to put an imaginary Mum into their stock statement, it has a profound effect. 'Thank you for calling (Mum),' 'Sorry, we don't deliver (Mum),' 'We are fully booked (Mum)'. Maybe we might make a bit of effort for our Mums.

SO WHY CUSTOMER CARE?

As I write this, it does seem that trouble is brewing once again. Actually as long as you don't flip to the front to find the copyright date, I will usually be 50 per cent right because it's always booming or busting, it's just that at the moment there is the acrid whiff of bust in the air. That means that our revenue stream will be drying up. That revenue stream is our customers. If they weren't our customers, they could be dead, skint or someone else's customers. We don't want the first two (unless we are morticians or insolvency lawyers) but the third we must fight to the death for. We must steal value from our competitors until they are drained, dried-out husks that crumble into dust and are destroyed, while we hang on to what we have. Our competitors cannot be stopped from stealing our ideas, encroaching on our markets or poaching our staff. A business guru famously tried to tie down what it was that our competitors couldn't steal. Well, he was a bit right. He said competitors could not steal our brand or our service. You could start making brown fizzy pop but you couldn't call it Coke. If your company has untouchably high levels of service, all your competition can do is to look on and weep. The best, the very best they can hope to do is to almost equal you. How can they overtake perfection?

BUT THE MANAGEMENT ARE TURDS

The cheery little bluebottle paddling around in this ointment is, firstly, that brand is a double-edged sword. What if your brand is synonymous with your being a total shit, cars that kill people and you know it, brutal exploitation of third world workers, and total disregard for the customer? I know lots of famous brands like that, do you? Secondly, service levels that can't be bettered. I don't know anyone like that. On the whole, I am not sure anyone gives a toss. A strange story involves a famous airline we use regularly. The cabin crew and check-in staff are consistent and often actively friendly and helpful. We had cause to deal with their senior management and in my opinion they are a bunch of complacent, arrogant turds.

Asking a member of their cabin crew what they thought of management, they replied 'We think they are a bunch of complacent, arrogant turds,' and, laughing, gave me a huge carrier bag full of miniatures and champagne to take home. Lions led by donkeys. Naturally intelligent people whose willingness is misdirected by crap management. Because of their sense of duty, ethics, dedication to safety (the nature of their job), conflict with the stupidity and naked greed of their bosses, they have become more loyal to the customers than to their company. This, in their case and ours, is good. They would happily waste fifty thousand pounds worth of company fuel to get you to a hospital should the need arise, but your staff should never be in that position.

A TEST DRIVE IN HIS PYJAMAS

In my previous books, I have given gee whiz examples of great service stories, and while researching this section, I have read a number of (mostly American) books on customer service. They have great heart-warming tales that make one say, 'Oh yes, that's right,' but I am a bit disturbed to find that I am not so keen on them this time. Look, try a few and see what you think. In one, I mention a Cadillac Garage in the US. A man couldn't sleep, he was so worried about the choice of colours on a seventy-thousand-dollar Cadillac he was thinking of buying. He woke his wife at 3.00 a.m. Sunday morning and she suggested ringing the garage there and then, saying that a security guard would be there and that he might be able to see which colours were in stock. The guard answered 'Thank you for calling us tonight, I'm Mike from Security. What can I do to help you?' 'What colour Eldorados do you have?' 'May I ask who is calling please, Sir?' 'Yes, my name is J B Schekenburger.' The security guard lights up a computer terminal to access customer records. 'Is that Mr JBJ Schekenburger the 15th of 157050053 Maple Drive?' 'It is.' 'Well Mr Schekenburger, it's kind of late at night now, would you like me to ring you back with the information now, or would you rather wait until the morning?' 'Oh, I got to know now!' 'My pleasure, Mr Schekenburger, I will be right back, and thank you for ringing me tonight.' It doesn't stop here because twenty minutes later, a smartly dressed and shaved salesman sweeps up Mr Schekenburger's drive with a shiny example of exactly the car he was looking for. That man took a test drive in his jimjams and slippers. It was the one he wanted, so a mechanic got out of bed to prepare the car, and it was parked ready to run in Mr Schekenburger's garage by breakfast time.

Apart from name changes and my lack of precise memory, this is a true story, one I have cheerfully bandied about to illustrate great service, but like the Beep Beep story, there is more than meets the eye. So let's do some digging.

At level one, this company are applying what I think is needed for survival. We are increasingly in a 24-hour, global society – it is always business hours somewhere in the world, and should be prepared to handle customers at any time. 'Sorry, we're closed', 'This branch is shut for staff training', 'There is no one to take your call at the moment, but your call is valuable to us.'

JUST A MOMENT

Oh, that sort of thing enrages me, doesn't it you? When you hear or see that, don't you immediately take your business and your money elsewhere? Do you have a phone message like that? I know I do – DOH!

A car can cost from ten to a hundred thousand pounds, and ten grand is enough in one hit. It is difficult to find someone to sell you one in normal trading hours, let alone outside them. What's the matter with us? Don't we want the business? I have a friend who transformed her ladies hairdressing business. How? She opened on Sundays. Now 40 per cent of her trade is done on a Sunday. That's a new 40 per cent, not just the old stuff spread about. She has stolen that business from her lazy, complacent competitors.

Next, the whole thing was kicked off by a security guard. The usual cheery response from security is 'there's no one 'ere, you'll 'ave to ring back'. Now if anyone needs a picture of his kids eating, he does. The customers' cash pays his wages too. Don't smile knowingly, it's your fault too. You create this nice cuddly bunny, 'we are the ones to love you and supply your needs' mission vision thing, and you have a security department whose only remit is to keep people out and set the dogs on them if they don't. They are part of your show, the chorus. There is no one who works for you – chairman or sweeper-up – that isn't involved in securing customers.

Again, another interesting point about this guard is that he has been trained to use the computer and access customer records.

That is creative thinking. Don't send him on dog provoking courses, but send him on sales, customer and IT courses. Think of it, a van driver who can sell, warehouse staff who can negotiate

– the list is endless – *but*, as we saw in the process re-engineering bit, we don't trust our people enough to let them become profit centres and start making us more money than they cost us. 'You can't trust a mere security guard to access confidential customer records and discuss sensitive issues. They are not of the correct calibre. You can't be sure they are trustworthy.'

Oh good, but they do have the run of the whole building all night, all the keys and the codes for the alarms. It's a good job they are too stupid to steal anything then, or you would be cleared out!

AND NOW THE BIG BUT

This tale of great 'customer is king' type service should get know-ing nods from the reader. The little smile, the sardonic eyebrow lift of recognition, at the Ah Ha-ness of it all, but now I'm worried be-cause that's what business books do. As mentioned earlier, I have been reading motivational business books recently, and they do have this effect. One just stated that the writer was in a shop to choose something. It was getting late, but he asked what time they closed. The answer was 'Sir, we are open for as long as you are here.' We all get that little warm feeling. My wife helps assemble these books and accuses me of being dark, destructive and nega-tive. Fair cop, but what's the point of a book like that? They are all full of these heart-warming little stories. Air stewards giving their kidneys to dying passengers with a cheery 'Have a nice day!' These books sell in millions but the real world is still dismally rude and uncaring. Get these twee little tales in your head, and then experience the High Street, the hotel, the steel stock holder, or airport check-in. Customer care has been bandied around for years. I see very little sign of it. Perhaps it doesn't matter after all. One of the busiest retailers I can think of has the worst service. They would be vulnerable however to a competitor with the same offer but better service, but you can't glue it on, you can't have staff dedicated to service whilst everyone else isn't. It has to be based on trust and example. Your enterprise must be like a stick of seaside rock which, wherever you cut it, will have 'service' written through every piece.

EVERYONE WHO WORKS WITH YOU, EMPLOYEES, SUB-CONTRACTORS, SUPPLIERS AND EVEN RELATIVES, ARE PART OF YOUR SHOW.

THINK
Disney would not tolerate a smelly man with a tray of dodgy pies walking through their park just because he is only a delivery guy from the baker's – 'he's nothing to do with us.'
- *It only takes one assassin to destroy your image.*
- *People who work with you will only behave well towards customers if they see you **really** think it is their most important task.*
- *If they have no power to say yes, then it doesn't work.*
- *The customer is your one and only source of income.*

THE GLOBAL MARKET

A TALE OF THE GLOBAL MARKET

Mr Amjolo sits outside his traditional village hut that he and his wife have fashioned from the local strong grasses and shrubs. A little of their precious wood has been used for strength and the mud walls are smoothed to perfection. Mr Amjolo's children have spent many days grinding white stones to a fine powder to make the walls reflect the strong sunlight. As Mr Amjolo puffs away at a pipe full of the pungent smoking herbs, he sees his cow, his goats, and a scattering of chickens. He is a happy man.

Then one day, out of the shimmering heat, comes a man – strangely dressed in a white suit and a wide-brimmed hat. He is carrying a smart leather case.

'Mr Amjolo?' the man asks. Mr Amjolo nods gently, still puffing at his pipe. 'How much of this area of land is yours?'

A strange request, but not one that Mr Amjolo feels any reason not to answer, and shielding his eyes with one hand, he points from horizon to horizon with the other.

'You see,' says the man walking to the tree that grows the bitter bean gourds, 'we are very interested in these'. Mr Amjolo is a little surprised. Sometimes his wife makes a sharp tasting drink with the beans, which is quite relaxing but is only really palatable with lots of wild honey and really isn't a patch on the strong grain wine the elders make. 'We would take ... I mean, purchase, as many of these as you could supply,' the man smiled.

Mr Amjolo, not forgetting his tradition of hospitality said 'Take them, friend, and go with my honour to you. That is all we have, but you are welcome to them. You have to pick them quickly, though, because the Embazzey worms eat them.'

The man looked at three pods, one of which was already serving as quite a feast to the Embazzey worms. 'No, you don't understand, we want tons of them, many many pods.'

'Then, friend, you must walk many miles and visit many villagers to collect so many pods.'

'No, you could cultivate them, plant them, harvest them, and we will give you rich rewards.'

Cultivate the bitter bean gourds, now that was a novel idea. Mind you, really cultivating anything was a fairly novel idea. The little bit of maize or millet sometimes needed a helping hand, like some seeds scattering once or twice a year. Sometimes the little extra could be swapped for cloth or tools. The animals more or less looked after themselves. For the family to harvest a little grain or catch a chicken for lunch was just part of the simple fun of life. 'Indeed,' thought Mr Amjolo, 'I am a happy man, but I would like rich rewards, maybe another cow, or some goats, or even a mule.' Out loud he asked 'What are these rich rewards?' The man opened a smaller leather case from his pocket and drew out a piece of green paper. There were pictures of stern men on this paper, some complicated patterns, but little else to impress. 'What is this?' Mr Amjolo asked.

'That is everything,' the man replied. 'That is currency, hard cash. Keep that one, by the way! You grow the bitter bean gourds, and we will give you many of these.'

'I don't understand, why should I swap something that is obviously valuable to you for bits of green paper? Quite nice, I suppose, but once you have seen one, you have seen them all.'

'No, you don't understand, the green paper has great value …'

'Who says?'

'Everyone in the world says.'

'I don't.'

'That's because you don't understand, Mr Amjolo. Because everybody in the world sees the green paper as valuable, it can be swapped for anything you want.'

'Anything?' Mr Amjolo had been eyeing the glittering jewel on the man's wrist. 'Can I swap my green paper for that?'

The man laughed. 'No, this is a Rolex, you would need many of those for one of these!'

'Why?'

'Because it takes valuable metal and many days of hard work to build one of these.'

'I think I see now,' said Mr Amjolo. 'They are sort of tokens for work.'

'Errm, well, I suppose so.' The man was growing impatient and didn't feel like giving a lecture on economics.

'Then what work do you do in your land that brings you such fine riches?'

He thought for a while and then only half joking said, 'We print the green paper.'

Mr Amjolo didn't completely understand but he liked the glittering jewel, so for a few days his family planted the bitter beans on a piece of ground that the goats didn't like. Time passed and he had what he considered a good pile of gourds, a lot of which had hardly been touched by the Embazzey worms.

The man returned, but did not seem over impressed by the crop. He did however give Mr Amjolo a bigger pile of the green pieces of paper. 'Can I now have that?' asked Mr Amjolo pointing at the jewel.

'Of course not, you need many times that before you have enough, but don't be sad, you do have enough for this.' The man produced a box of bottles, one of which he opened. Mr Amjolo and the man took it in turns to drink. It was certainly smoother and more pungent than the elders' brew. Soon his head was spinning.

'Mass cultivation,' the man was slurring slightly, 'That's what you need, mass cultivation using mechanisation. You could grow from here to here.' It was now the man's turn to point from horizon to horizon.

Mr Amjolo wasn't that drunk. 'It would take a thousand men.'

'Or one tractor,' smiled the man.

'Tractor?'

'A machine that does the work of men. It never rests and has great power.'

'Where can I get such a great machine?'

'We can send you one.'

'Such a wonderful thing must cost more than even that jewel. I have not got the green paper.'

'We will lend you the green paper, and when the tractor has made you rich, you can pay us back.' Mr Amjolo had a sly thought. It would be possible if the man was not truthful that he would never be rich and would never have to give the green paper back, but he was a very honest person and he told the man his thoughts. 'You see,' said the man, 'we add a thing called interest. So for each year you don't pay us, we add a little bit more to what you owe us, so if you leave it too long, you may owe us a lot.'

Mr Amjolo smiled to himself. What did it matter how much was owed – if he couldn't pay, he couldn't pay and anyway, it was only bits of green paper. He shook hands with the man and made his mark on some white paper.

A few weeks later, a big red tractor appeared and the man showed him how to use it. Soon horizon to horizon was filled with the bitter bean gourd plants. Mr Amjolo and his family toiled night and day to harvest the gourds and they gathered a huge pile of them, a lot of which had not been eaten by the Embazzey worms.

The man returned and smiled at the great pile of gourds. 'That tractor is a truly powerful machine. Do you make them in your land?' asked Mr Amjolo.

'We used to, but our people are far too clever and valuable to be wasted on building tractors. We have taught lesser people in far-off lands to make them.'

'Do those people get my bitter beans?'

'No, they get green paper.'

'Do they buy my bitter beans with the green paper?'

'Well your bitter beans are used for luxury products which I'm sure the people in far-off lands would like, but at the moment they must use the green paper to pay the people in our land who own their tractor factories, and who must be paid for knowing the secrets of tractor building.'

'What do you make in your land, then?'

'We make thoughts and green paper.'

'So is everybody clever?'

'No, of course not.'

'Do those people who are not clever have goats and grow your crops?'

'No, they wear hats made of paper and they prepare food for the people that make green paper, special food that can be eaten while the green paper makers hurry from one place to another.' The man was looking at the huge pile of gourds.

'Am I rich?' asked Mr Amjolo

'Well, of course we must withhold the stage payment, and the price is severely curtailed by the worm infestation.' With that, he handed over a disappointingly small pile of green paper.

'The worms are part of life. With so little reward, I am working for you and the worms.'

'Spray!'

'Spray?'

'I will give you a liquid that will kill the worms. By the way, is there anything else you need?'

'Some more of your bottles. My wife enjoys them very much. They do worry me because she drinks them, sleeps and forgets to cook for us, but then she says it makes her happy.'

'If she likes it, there's no problem and we can let you have our food that needs no cooking.'

'Do I have to wear a paper hat?'

'No, but it helps.'

Mr Amjolo sprayed, and the worms died. His youngest son also became very sick, perhaps because he slept near the tins of spray.

The man came back, saw the mountain of gourds and was pleased, but he still only gave Mr Amjolo a disappointingly small pile of green paper. The man explained. 'We had to charge you for the interest, the spray, the booze and the food, but you are getting the hang of it now. To make some extra profit, why not plant these and get rid of the goats? They are eating your crop.' The man had pointed to Mr Amjolo's maize crop.

'I need my maize and I need my goats and your spray has made my child sick.'

'We gave you great food, so you don't need the goat or the maize, and your kid has an allergy. We can supply medicine.'

Mr Amjolo did what the man said and the crop grew, but he never seemed to be ahead of the game. The man always found an excuse for not handing over the green paper. In the meantime, his neighbours had been similarly trapped by the man and had nothing to trade. Although they didn't all get along too well because of old family feuds, they decided to gather together and print their own green paper which they could swap amongst each other. When the man returned, Mr Amjolo showed him their green paper and offered to pay the man off. The man threw back his head and roared with laughter. 'Your green paper is worthless!'

'Why?'

'Because I say so.'

'Why is yours worth so much?'

'Because I say so.'

Mr Amjolo was starting to dislike the man. He wished he had never met him and that he could have his old life back. Then one day a stranger came. He said he came from far-off lands, but he had a jewel on his wrist just like the man. The stranger asked Mr Amjolo if he would like the jewel. Mr Amjolo had been caught like this before and asked with great suspicion 'How much?'

'One or two pieces of green paper, or just one sack of those,' said the stranger, pointing to the bitter gourds. Mr Amjolo was delighted, the jewel even said 'Rolex' on it.

When the first man came again and saw Mr Amjolo wearing the jewel he was very angry. 'Where did you get that?' he demanded. Mr Amjolo explained, and was also quite angry because the man had tried to cheat him over the jewel. 'But that isn't a real one, it's a copy!' said the man.

'It is exactly the same, it glitters, it ticks and it predicts the height of the sun in the sky, it even says Rolex.'

'That's the point,' the man said, 'It shouldn't say Rolex. It's called branding. It means we must be allowed to charge what we like for our products.' Then he calmed down a little and said 'By the way, we don't need the gourds at the moment, there is a global oversupply, but good luck selling them elsewhere.'

'But without the green paper, we cannot eat, we grow no crops we can eat because of your gourds. The tractor is broken and we need expensive parts, and your spray made my child sick and now we need your expensive medicine. Doesn't it make your children sick?'

'Actually that spray is banned in our land, and our big chemical companies have to sell it somewhere, but I must warn you that the interest is still building up.'

Mr Amjolo finally cracked. 'You are the devil. We sold our souls for your green paper and your stupid gourds. You are lazy people. You make nothing, and I have worked a great deal. We will swap the accursed gourds with the people in the far-off land for the useful things they make. Your global economy will destroy you. You can shove your green paper and may the burden of my debt, and that of all those like me, crush you like the insects you so cheerfully poison.'

The man returned to his own land, and to his horror he found that Mr Amjolo's warning had become true. The value of all the man's bits of paper fell and fell, and too late he realised he couldn't live in a world where someone else always did the work. Like Mr Amjolo, he thought he would go back to the simple things. Then he discovered that his people had tried to produce animals and crops in the same way that they had used to produce tractors in big factories. The animals and the crops had produced horrifying new diseases and had given people a madness that only death released them from. The young people were either arrogant and thoughtless or were in despair because they were tired of wearing paper hats and smiling at people who treated them with contempt. None of them knew how to do anything. It was much harder to forge iron or fashion wood than it was to throw a colour television together. Every day the green numbers became red because the truth was nothing had real value. The man was ruined and broken and lay in the rain waiting for death. He lay in the rain because he didn't even have the simple skill to build a hut like Mr Amjolo.

So, the baddy gets it. A happy ending – but sadly not, because the man in the far-off land discovered that if he made tractors, phones, televisions, and computers faster, he could make them cheaper and give his people prosperity. He got faster and cheaper until he had built a tractor, a phone, a television, and a computer for everyone in the world. Soon he was filling sheds with these things, and offering them at a loss, but who wants two computers? He went and lay in the rain.

Mr Amjolo could never get back his soul. His land was ruined by overspraying, his wife had to have the bottle or she saw snakes that weren't there. The tractor never ran again, and the children went hungry. Mr Amjolo lay down and hoped for rain.

THE TRUTH

The way to make money is to take something that is cheap to us, and then to brutally drive it cheaper at the expense of its producer. We then need people to add as much value as possible to this thing, while paying them as little as we can get away with. The final step is to tempt and tantalise someone to pay the biggest amount for it with no danger of comeback or refund. If you doubt this, imagine the pay levels of the sweated labour digging up the brown earth called bauxite, through to the stitching up we get when an oily git sells us this processed earth as an aluminium conservatory. We may feel a little miffed when we start to see our multi-thousand-pound investment as a few pennies worth of smelted earth.

A brutal description maybe, but it is how we all make our living whether it is products that we make, or services we offer where we actually add value to thin air. I know the benign hippies among us would be outraged at the slur that they indulge in any of this, but even things like fair trade coffee schemes really aren't that fair, and work on the simple premise that if your peasant growers starve to death then they won't be able to be used next year. Anyway, who pays the surcharge on ethical produce? You guessed it, the gubbins with the smelted earth conservatory. The true cynic might describe it as a marketing ploy.

The story of Mr Amjolo, however, does signpost some pitfalls that we need to avoid.

The first threat is that the raw material supplier is driven so low that they die. This isn't just Mr Amjolo, it is any supplier. I know of a major retailer that pays its buyers a good basic wage, and then adds a 100 per cent bonus that depends on one simple thing. They must always pay a lower price this year than they did last year, even if it is .00001 per cent less, that is enough, but the pressure is always on. The argument is that it makes the supplier efficient, but you can only get so efficient and then you get squeezed. Consider this: you are a caring employer against all I said in my previous tirade, and you manufacture teddy bears in Sheffield, England. By careful purchasing of raw materials, and a dedication to quality and control of waste, the business is tightly and efficiently run. Your production is a total of ten thousand man hours a week, at an average of ten pounds per hour. That is one hundred thousand pounds a week. Your nearest competitor, who also vies for the superstores' business, moves all production to distant lands where his costs are less than a pound an hour, or ten thousand pounds a week.

THOUGHT

Again, this is a case of departmental objectives that conflict with the extended success of the enterprise. Trust, honesty and partnership with suppliers might be a good idea.

THE THIRD WORLD IS HERE

I was having dinner with a group of financial barons, one of whom was one of the shadowy people that controls the country's finances. I put this point to him and asked him for the solution. The reply was 'We shouldn't be making teddies here. Designing them, marketing them, rebranding them, tying them to themed Hollywood teddy movies, yes, but not making them.' He went on to explain that as other people did our dirty work, of course they would become more skilled. Yesterday they shovelled earth, today they smelt aluminium, tomorrow they build computer controlled extruders, but we shouldn't worry because it just pushes us up the food chain to more esoteric and cerebral pursuits, like designing sub-photon computer chips and genetic engineering. 'But there are millions of people who could never design computer chips. What do they do?' I asked. I suggested that the third world wasn't in the far-off places anymore but was the bottom third of our own society, the third that wouldn't even get the dubious pleasure of working in a teddy bear factory. The social reformers who can't face the truth of this statement think that everyone could be educated to design computers or whatever. Decide the logic of that one yourself. The answer lies with us, the business dynamos, who as always will use our pragmatic desire for commerce to solve this one.

LET THEM ADD VALUE

The next threat is from the work force, which if it feels too crushed or used, can turn quite nasty. To be truthful, if you don't pay enough, they can start off pretty nasty too. Another thing is that we tend to focus on job descriptions and whatnot and forget that in the money making chain, the people who work with us should be adding value. Managers, because they have got nothing better to do, are obsessed with process and not outcome. Because of this, they tend to concentrate on the minutiae and not the big picture. In a book I wrote on being self employed, I stated that that was one of the biggest problems the self-employed faced. If you can release your management from this bond, life would be truly cheery. Say you sold tables for five hundred pounds, you could give a fifty pound lump of wood to someone and say 'Bring it back as a table. If it is precisely this quality, I will pay you one hundred pounds.' End of story, but we can't bear it. We would rather tolerate poor quality so we can say, 'How much time have you taken off? How did you achieve the results, how many hours are you booking to this?' and so on.

THINK ABOUT …

… Whoever you employ, look at them as a complete business with a profit and loss account. Pay them £500 and if they return £550, you can't lose. As a last resort, leave it to them to justify their existence.

HOW THIS BOOK GOT WRITTEN

If you have never written a book, you will not know what curmudgeonly and demanding people publishers are, and I have just had quite a tricky few moments with mine. You see, publishers follow a lot of the above mentioned rules, making inordinately huge sums of money from the sweat of their authors' brows and the outpourings of their tortured minds. They take a few pence worth of paper and trap an unsuspecting genius into creating a magnum opus on it. For this, they expect the punters to part with millions of pounds at such places as airport book stalls, but they also fall into the trap of process rather than outcome. In other words, they tend to look over one's shoulder.

I suppose to be fair, I must put forward their argument, which is that they give cash advances to a bunch of feckless tossers in the hope that they will return some time in the future with a book, whereas in reality they tend to take the money and bugger off with it. To prevent this, the publisher likes to view the work in stages. Hence the row! Mine has just viewed this stage and on threat of having his money back, I was summoned to his lair. My footsteps echoed off the marble of his huge vaulted office, that in any horror movie could have been the evil one's sepulchre. He crouched, insect-like, behind the huge desk, surrounded by documents, bags of cash, and jars containing human organs. Legend has it that one of these jars contained his own heart.

'What's this Amjolo stuff? You are a depressing git. You are supposed to be a business motivation writer. Be cheerful and optimistic, or give me my money back.'

Nervously turning my hat in my trembling hands, and staring down at my dusty shoes, I replied 'We are all doomed, but don't take back the money, my children need food.'

'The readers buy this sort of book because it gives them optimism for the future. It should suggest japes and wheezes that will make them a success.'

I take his point, but I always find motivational books to be on fairly dodgy ground. They have this cheery 'if you want to get there, you shouldn't start from here' view of things. Self-belief, happy, motivated staff, wonderful customers, in a world of unbounded opportunity.

A very sad tale that always brings the problem with this home to me, is that when rescuers got to the overturned ferry, the Herald of Free Enterprise, they saved a small girl from the flooded and darkened interior of the stricken ship. She kept weeping 'Why did this happen? I have been good, like Mummy and Daddy told me.' The positive thinking brigade have a similar innocent view, but I believe there is no harm in a bit of negative thinking. The global market, along with its vicious competition, is going to be eye-wateringly tough, but if you know that, then you can prepare and even prosper.

If you buy a road atlas, you wouldn't want a positive one that when you looked up the mileage charts, said things like 'nearer than you thought,' or 'just a step away'. Maybe they would lie about distances or hills so as not to depress you. I even read one motivational book that said 'Don't watch the news, it will demotivate you!' If a good sailor sees storm clouds gathering he can make preparation to ensure his survival, however difficult the conditions become. If I had been designing the Titanic, I would have put lots and lots of lifeboats on it, because I believe anything can sink.

MESSAGE
It isn't negative thinking to be honest about the problems that face us, it's just stupid not to – otherwise seat belts would be called 'expecting a crash negative thinking restraints'.

DISMAL GITS RULE OK

I have wandered alone (but successful) in the wilderness until my fellow gurus found a trendy management name for being a dismal git. I am rehabilitated, I am an exponent of 'positive negativity' or better still, 'constructive pessimism'.

We must look at the threats and opportunities in the early part of this chapter and then, while being aware of the dangers, we can make serious money.

HOW TO RULE THE WORLD

I got a call from a company who invited me to speak at their international conference in some exotic tropical location (my kind of conference). When I get these calls, I like to know as much as possible about the intended victims. This investigation is conducted in the guise of a briefing, so ostensibly I can customise my presentation, but it is really to ascertain how nasty they could turn, and whether I might be in any personal danger (the audience were with me all the way, but I shook them off at Birmingham). The client told me that the audience would consist of 500 of their employees. This global company was very successful and had a turnover of 500 million dollars.

'How many people do you employ worldwide?' I asked
'500.'

'500? Do you mean that the whole company is going to be there?'

'Of course.'

A stunning revelation came to me. 'Hang on a minute, that means you are getting one million dollars of turnover from each employee.'

'That's right.'

What they did, was 'make' hydraulics and pneumatics for process industries from pharmaceuticals to aircraft manufacturers. It struck me that everybody at the conference was either sales or sales support.

'Where do you manufacture?'

'We don't manufacture, everything is made by subcontractors.'

The designs are sent to subcontractors who are based all over the world and are often duplicated to serve local markets. It is the perfect outcome-driven management structure. Quality and quantity issues are dealt with at a stroke. 'I sell it for ten pounds, you make it for four pounds. We will reject any that don't come up to standard, some months we need a thousand, others ten thousand.'

Why on earth, when you look at this logically, would you ever have production in-house? Quality issues are a nightmare because you have to keep beating your own employees over the head to stop the reject and scrap items, which you then have the problem of disposing of.

'So,' I said 'That is very clever. They make your product and you assemble and distribute them.'

'No, we don't assemble or distribute. ' At this point he mentioned one of the very well known parcel and distribution companies. 'They do it all, they have even built a special warehouse to handle our work.'

Even their spare parts scheme was cunning. The part number on the components and in the parts list contained a code which had to be used when dialling for spares. This number would route you straight to the subcontractor who had made the components. I know you can already sense the potential for cock ups and fiddles, but I must remind you that the essence of this book, if there is one, is to get other people to do your work, and like the security guard, the warehouse man, and the peasants, we have to get them to be great and then trust them. Part of the subcontractor's contract was to answer the phone correctly and to charge the catalogue price for parts unless they were faulty, in which case they would supply them free of charge.

'Then where is your head office?' I asked

They thought long and hard. 'We don't really have a HEAD office. We all do our work out of our own offices, or for that matter, no office,' one laughed, waving a laptop and a mobile phone.

One of the cleverest things that they had done was on the recruitment of their sales people. They didn't look for people who know about pneumatics or hydraulics, but instead recruited people from the industries and areas they wanted to sell to. If Fred was a Peruvian helicopter maker, it stood to reason he had chums in the Peruvian aerospace industry, contacts with the military and an intimate knowledge of all the political and bureaucratic pitfalls. You could teach him about hydraulics. The company's flexibility was astonishing. One South American country had an 80 per cent import duty. Within a day they had found subcontractors and were making the product there and slaughtering the competition. They were told that a Far Eastern manufacturer had been ripping off their designs, some of them came into their hands, and they were disturbed to find that the products were perfect copies. They went to see this manufacturer, who laughed and told them that no Western company had successfully sued in his country.

'What did you do?' I asked.

'He is now our local manufacturer and distributor; after all, he was doing a great job.'

So what have we got? We have a true global company and a true virtual company. If we had the courage we could all do that. At the end of everyone's telephone line lies production capacity worth billions of pounds. You could be a multi-million-pound company before teatime. Go on, I dare you.

World domination is possible from your back bedroom. It is now a level playing field and companies of any size can be global players, bu do you have the nerve to do it?

SOME NEW OLD IDEAS

There was another unseemly and degrading tussle with my publisher when, whilst he was giving me a Chinese burn to recover his cheque, I managed to sink my teeth into the ageing flesh of his upper arm.

'Listen, we want some ground-breaking new stuff or I want my money back,' he said, through gritted teeth.

Well I think global trading and virtual companies are pretty cutting-edge stuff, but like all new ideas, when you look at them they are probably some very old ideas with flash names. Customer care is CRM, process re-engineering is 'Fast' companies, close that sale is Relationship Selling. Maybe the same could be said about the global virtual company. At the risk of being sued, it may be fair to say that Coca-Cola is brown fizzy pop made to a secret recipe. If you had the recipe and a clean bucket you could make it and, if the owners of the name let you use the name, you could sell the stuff. Therefore all over the world, people with clean buckets and the correct licenses are making and selling famous western brands. Bingo – a virtual, global company. Cigarettes, hamburgers, beers and fizzy drinks, have been doing it for years. Perhaps we should ask why they bother to make or do anything themselves? The logical conclusion of this would be to discover that Mr McDonald runs the whole empire from his back bedroom and the only clue that his neighbours have that he is a global magnate is his mop of bright orange hair and huge red shoes.

There have been millions of words written recently on global branding – to be fair, there have been sodding great riots about it, with all the gurus from both right and left gazing intently up their own bottoms. Unfortunately my own bottom is not such a receptacle of esoteric knowledge, and also – bearing in mind the blood curdling threats of my publisher – perhaps we could take a more pragmatic and practical view. How can we be global players and make wads of lovely wonga from this? A good place to start, don't you think?

BUY THE BRAND, STUFF THE PRODUCTION

My son delights, and has delighted for a number of years, in coming back from dodgy foreign climes with fake products, particularly watches. A few years ago these products were a complete
joke. In the case of the watches, they carried the famous name
but that was about all. They were made of clearly inferior metals,
with garish colours and cheap electronic movements, but recently
they have improved to the point that the last one I saw was what I
would describe as a perfect copy. I own the real version of this
particular Swiss watch, and the copy is indistinguishable from it.
The movement is automatic, it has mineral crystal glass and is
made of heavy stainless steel. A thousand-pound watch for twenty pounds. That isn't a bit cheaper, not half the price, it is a fiftieth
of the price. Of course, the real owner of the brand goes absolutely
apeshit and has big displays of fakes being crushed with steam
rollers, etc. The situation is even worse with copyright products
like software, films and music, where you can buy almost any
software, or the latest movie on DVD, in streetmarkets for pennies. The dodge for us of course is that this can work rather nicely
in reverse. If you can get hold of a brand or product that is struggling, you could have the product built for a fiftieth of the current
cost, and then flog it back here at the usual price. Just look at what
the West has lost: Norton motorcycles, Riley cars, De Haviland
aircraft. I know some of the above-mentioned are probably sitting
on a shelf somewhere, ready to go again, but I am more interested
in the ones that haven't gone yet.

THOUGHT

*If you own a famous brand or if you have great salespeople, produc-
tion can be done anywhere by anybody.*

I have a small engineering workshop just to satisfy my personal proclivities, and I have a treasured British-built lathe. A new replacement for this would cost £5000, a Chinese copy would cost £800. The only problem is that the Chinese version doesn't function as accurately, but after £400 worth of skilful fettling it works as well as its dearer rival. 'Why do the British company bother building them in England at all?' I laughed, until I looked at the plate on my latest machine, and saw that they didn't.

BEWARE OBSOLETE PEOPLE

Now is the time to put my hippie hat on again, and have a little worry. You, my friendly reader chum, could do this tomorrow. You are a few phone calls away from being a car maker, a ship builder, watch maker, or a builder of prestige hi-fi equipment. People who buy, and even more rarely read, business books (you got this far, so this means you) are by definition quite bright, probably in the top 5 per cent when it comes to nous, and without a doubt in the top 20 per cent. You are probably taking a bored flick through these pages as you sip Chablis from a flute glass in your business class seat as you are wafted at 30,000 feet to your next urgent meeting. I have no doubt you could be a global player. The small globe has levelled the playing field so the fast-thinking small player can take on the world. Sit back and enjoy the trip, you are equipped to succeed, but the guy who is currently nicking your car from the executive long-term car park is not. He should have been bashing those red-hot rivets, or running those lathes, but you can't afford him anymore. As I have said, the third world isn't out there, it's here, it's the bottom third of our society that is effectively obsolete. Oh boy, that really disturbs me. Obsolete people. Despite every effort, there is no solution. If it is cheaper to make your teddies in Taiwan, then you must do that or go under. Some people suggest that education is the answer but there are two jumbo problems with that. One just assumes that everyone has the same potential and you turn every college, driving school and scout hut into a university. You return to the dilemma that the man from the far-off lands had, and that is over-production. Ten million lawyers, ten million HR specialists, ten million anything – clever, but we just won't need them at all. You pick up the phone today and get laptops made in wherever for £10 each, and sell them here for £2000. Sell a million a year with the help of your mum and one of your kids. The profit is billions, the corporation tax is billions. Why not stash some in a glittering skyscraper that can be your self administered pension and for your ego's sake, if not for tax reasons, fill it with staff – HR, Marketing, Purchasing, Catering, you will have them all. Everyone with a glittering degree. Be scared, be ready to weep because the frightening thing is, they don't know that they are just your playthings. They go to conferences, and discuss psychometric testing and paradigm shifts, but if your competition get close, you could chop the lot. To reiterate the origin of this chapter, you buy cheap, you pay low, you sell high, you become rich. Everything else is faldey-da and bullshit. That makes me uneasy because my heart tells me that every human has a right to have a life of value, and just mopping up the spare cash from exploitation, however it is wrapped, is not my idea of a valuable career. Oh yes, and second, not everyone however non-PC this sounds, has got the potential for intellect-based further education. Hey, I know, lets lower the standards then no one will feel left out!

BE A SQUIRREL

There is no solution that I can see, and I suppose that I must advise you to fill your boots before someone else does. I have a personal solution that I call 'Red Squirrel'. I am sure that you are mentally fit, eager, and raring to go (you had better be). The battle will be fierce and you will fight it every minute of ever day, moving prod-ucts, being aware of trends, spotting people who may be sharper, quicker, and more competitive than you. This is all about speed. The fast win, the faster win more, the fastest wins it all. I do it. I fight fast and hard, but it's like swimming in a fierce current. It's tiring, but your life depends upon it. I should imagine that those who drown must be almost relieved to be able to stop struggling, but there is an alternative.

The squirrel population of the UK was once red. Red squir-rels are gentle, uncompetitive, relaxed little creatures, so when the ferociously competitive grey squirrels were introduced they drove the red squirrels out. They competed for food, habitat, and space. The battle was totally one-sided, but not a tragedy. Rather than fighting to the death or being subjugated by the grey squir-rels, the red squirrels just buggered off. No hassle, no worries or bitterness: 'You want it that much, you have it.' They can be found on secluded islands and in isolated woods, doing their gentle, squirrelly things. As the pressure builds and you count the scars you picked up fighting for every nut or acorn, consider the red squirrel alternative. Of course you will have made your pile, the bank balance will be healthy, but before you consider next year's expansion plans, go to a Mediterranean harbour and look at that middle-aged couple on the wooden schooner. They both have skins like crocodile-hide handbags, and are discussing the winter voyage to Tobago. Or look at that Harley-mounted Hell's Angel floating across Arizona with his entire belongings strapped to the rack and a terrier wearing a flying helmet sitting on the petrol tank. The shock when he takes off the crash helmet to reveal the grey hair. The pair of Buddhist beach bums on Lantau Island in Hong Kong who strangely arrive at the beach each day in a vin-tage Rolls Royce. These are the red squirrels – not drowned, just living elsewhere. Why be in the rat race if you are not a rat?

- *We make money from the efforts of other people.*
- *Anyone can be a global player.*
- *If you have the brand, you can produce anywhere.*
- *If you can sell, you can produce anywhere.*
- *For your own sanity, consider the people you exploit.*
- *When you have made your pile, consider stopping and becoming human again.*

GRAVEL – AN AFTERTHOUGHT

I recently worked with a company that quarried gravel. It sells for £9 a ton, costs £6 per ton to move and £25 a ton to import. So, there are alternatives to globalisation – some businesses, gravel, rocks, building, haulage, water, etc. It's just finding one that no one else has thought of.

EVERYONE CAN SELL – EVERYONE SHOULD SELL

5

As we have been seeing, we can all work fast, make cutting-edge high-quality products for a fraction of our competitors' costs, and build a workforce that is enthusiastic, loyal and cheap. We are still knackered because the great new millennium company has completely forgotten how to sell. The trouble with great new ideas is that they tend to chuck out all the old great ideas. Strangely enough I have a rather inexplicable interest in steam engines. This is of no import other than to mention that I have very old books on the technical science of steam engines. If you think a book on computer design is tricky, try one of these huge tomes on valve movements, particularly the ones from the start of the twentieth century. This technology was highly advanced and complex, but we have discarded it. In business, particularly in the 1950s and 1960s, huge works were penned on the science of selling. This too has been discarded – perhaps rightly so. Death of a Salesman, commercial travellers, sample cases, Ford Cortinas, sales trainers in white suits – all very depressing stuff that should be incinerated along with the mustard trevira flares, but let's salvage one truthful formula from that time.

PRODUCTION MINUS SALES EQUALS SCRAP

Those awful hairy-chested medallion men who pounded our motorways in their Fords and Vauxhalls, and whose idea of nirvana was a promotion that would result in a Ford Granada, those people could actually sell their employers out of any corner. Look at the products of the fifties, sixties, seventies: they were crap! It was only the salesforce that held back the tide. We sold dodgy ships, cars and aircraft to the world. As the salesmen and their skills died, the dam of confidence they built died with them and we were inundated. Let's imagine that if we took our IT skills, our trim staff, and globally sourced innovative products and services, and then added the lost art of selling, the world would be ours. Global domination within our grasp. A modest and achievable goal.

THOUGHT

At the time, a great deal of work and effort went into old methods and technologies and it is worth digging out ancient business books and reading them. You will also have the added benefit of hind-sight.

WE DON'T SELL ANYMORE

We don't currently sell to our customers. Apparently we have a relationship with them. As you may have noticed in my tirade on customer care, I don't think there is any (customer care, that is), but no matter, we now have CRM – Customer Relationship Management – a bit of lunacy that I shall rant about elsewhere, but bear in mind just for now that the modern art of CRM is strictly one way. Brutally translated, this means call centres, where we – the customers – ring companies and if we are so upset that we quietly bugger off, they never get to hear of it. The relationship in this case is most certainly not proactive. There is a kind of terrifying osmotic bleed through from one loony modern culture to the next. In this loopy, politically-correct world of ours, the politicians, the social workers and the counsellors have a real thing about rela-tionships, and because commerce likes to be seen as 'right on' and up to speed, 'relationships' have arrived for us too. A classic example is 'Relationship Selling'. That is a bit like having a vegetarian abattoir.

I am sometimes invited to undertake one-to-one coaching for sales staff, and recently an incident brought this incongruity into focus. I was in a car with a salesman who was not achieving the correct level of success with his calls. We stopped outside a glittering tower.

'What are we doing here?' I asked.

'One of our best customers,' he replied. 'We have a great relationship.'

'Great!' I cheered, 'What are you going to sell them today?'

Panic ensued. My companion stared about wildly as if we were being observed. 'SHHHH!' he hissed. 'We don't want to sell them anything.'

'Why not?'

'Don't want to spoil the relationship.'

'So what are you doing here?'

'Building bridges, forging links.'

BEAT THE TRUTH OUT OF THEM

Strangely enough I can understand his desire not to upset the customer, but just because the customer has not expressed an emotion, it doesn't mean that they haven't got one. Somewhere else in this book I mentioned the annoying practice of approaching diners in a restaurant and asking, 'S'everything awright wif your meal?' to which nearly all of us reply 'Yes, thank you very much,' despite the fact that we would secretly vow never to eat there again.

As I said, I generated huge consternation by suggesting that we pick the customer up by the throat and say 'Are you seriously suggesting that this is the best meal you have ever eaten?' Of course that is provocative. Of course the answer will be 'no', but then it gives us the chance to ask the question that will let us know what sort of hill we have to climb.

'Why? What was wrong with it?'

'The fries could have been hotter, the meat was a bit tough, the slug in the salad put up a hell of a fight!' It's our road map thing again. If we don't know the true challenge of the journey, however difficult or arduous, it is unlikely that we can complete it.

THOSE TOUGH QUESTIONS

I am intrigued by the idea that we can make success inevitable and I would like to talk to you about targeted selling and intending to sell. In other words, you pick the people you would like to do business with, and you will do business with them, but you must uncover the facts and real obstacles. The truth is that once revealed, the obstacles may be so big that the rewards may not be worth the cost in effort. The trouble is that we fear the truth, so by avoiding asking about it, we think that it isn't there. A classic example is the way we lose key and established accounts. CRM be buggered – when did you last ring a customer and ask directly the tough question about how happy they are with you? I don't mean customer satisfaction surveys because they suck. What I do mean is you picking up the phone and saying 'Are we the best supplier you have ever done business with?' You drive an expensive car, live in a nice house, when did that car manufacturer ring and ask you if you liked every aspect of the car, or the builder about your house, the plumber about the last repair or installation he did for you? Don't fall into the trap of saying 'Yeah, but the car is five years old.' That is just the point because the longer you have been loyal and uncomplaining, the less inclined the supplier is to bother with you. Of course the irony is that it is about this time you are looking to change. This can be carried over into selling by understanding that these hidden truths that drive away our current customers can be the same or similar truths that prevent them doing business with us in the first place. On the whole, people are sensitive and polite and don't wish to upset us with unpleasant truths.

For example, 'I have no intention of buying from you,' is expressed as 'That's very nice. I'll pop back when I've done the rest of my shopping.' We have got to dig deep for the real facts and this digging can be quite confrontational. I would describe selling as a gentle and subtle art, so this next bit might come as something as a shock, but let us get the viciousness and confrontation over with before the more sophisticated stuff.

TRY THIS

Ring all your customers, even ones that go back many years. You will be amazed at the amount of business that is generated.

HAPPY, FRIENDLY PEOPLE RARELY BUY

Therefore turn them into miserable, argumentative gits and they might buy.

Some time ago, I used to give presentations to small and start-up companies, and their dream was to win that big order or contract from one of the major players. All they wanted, they said, was to have that door opened for them, just once. One particular person was starting an office cleaning company, and would gaze wistfully at the glittering headquarters of a huge insurance company.

'Just one shot at them, that's all I need,' he would sigh.

'Just what would this one shot consist of?' I asked

'Well, if I had your gift of the gab, I could get an appointment with someone senior instead of the gatekeeper who keeps me away the whole time.'

'Would you like me to make your dream come true? I have just done a conference for their CEO and he owes me one. Would you like me to make you an appointment?'

The answer was mouth-frothingly positive. I duly made the appointment with the most powerful man in this company, and I sent our friend on his dream appointment. He came back full of it. 'What a nice man, surprisingly approachable.'

'What did you sell him?'

I know it's a bit like that relationship selling story and the answer was just as disappointing. 'Nothing yet, but he was very interested.'

'Very interested' is a sort of clichéd phrase that will occur time and time again and has nothing to do with anybody being interested – very or otherwise. It is the easiest thing for the failed salesperson to write in their reports. 'Went to see buyer, Acme Industries, liked our idea. Very interested, will consult Board and call us soon.' The more experienced and blasé have condensed all this load of old flannel into 'V.INT'. To make all this a bit clearer, why don't we listen in to our hero's dream appointment?

The scene. The great man's office. He is pouring over vital documents that only happen to look a little like Golf World magazine. A gentle tapping is heard at the door, a little too gentle for the great man to hear. The tapping comes a little louder, and even a little louder. 'Come in!' his greatness shouts. The door opens a crack and our friend peers in. 'Ah, you must be the chap that Geoff told me about. Come in, come in. Do sit down. Cigar?'

After a bit of confusion with hand shaking, dropped briefcases, scattered papers, knocked over ornaments, and a very, very polite refusal to the offer of the cigar, the dance begins.

'Geoff tells me you have started a cleaning business and would like to tell me about it. Well fire away, tell me all about yourself.'

'Well, your greatness, me an' the missus started this up when I was made redundant from the abattoir.'

'Marvellous, how enterprising.'

'My brother-in-law designed these brochures in his anger therapy classes!'

'Lovely, and such vivid colours.'

This goes on for the whole of the allocated 30 minutes, then: 'Thank you so much for sharing all this with me. I do so hope you do well. I could listen to your fascinating story all day but I hope you understand I have a board meeting to go to, so we must wrap things up.'

'Of course, your grand mightiness, and thank you for sparing me so much of your time.'

Very interested? A total disaster and a waste of the favour I called in. To make matters worse, that blown opportunity means that there will be no chance of a second chance. What possible reason could there be to see this man again? Now what I am going to suggest is for this demonstration only, and it flies in the face of every accepted sales technique inasmuch as we are going to intentionally piss off the potential customer, so don't try this at home, and if you do, don't blame me.

The scene, the same. The knocking the same.

'Ah, you must be the chap that Geoff told me about. Come in, come in, do sit down.'

'I have come here because I would like to ask you for the contract to clean this place.'

'We have someone to do that already.'

'I am sure you have, but I think I would do a better job. Will you give the work to me?'

'No.'

'Why not?'

Getting annoyed: 'Because I don't know you from Adam.'

'When you do know me better, can I have the work?'

'No, how do I know you will do the job?'

'You could speak to our current customers. They will tell you how good we are.'

'I don't think you are big enough to handle our work.'

'Is that all that is stopping you from giving us the job?'

'No.'

'So what else worries you?'

Very aggressive, horribly abrasive, but the truth is coming out. The potential customer has a huge list of worries about why he shouldn't buy. He didn't express any of these worries before, because he was under no threat of buying. He could be as nice as pie because there was no intention to buy.

THE POINT

This short tale is to illustrate that our potential customers' resistance to our offer exists in their heads and that we must get it out in the open before we know where we are. If we don't know where we are, we can't start our journey. The flash name for this is *ESTABLISHING OUR POSITION*. That is vital, even if that position is up shit creek. There is no point in kidding yourself.

GET THEM ALL AT IT

My intention within the general theme of this book is to get everyone doing it, whatever it may be. We will have a glimpse-ette at sophisticated sales techniques, but the real value is to get everyone selling. Just imagine the implications if every contact or point of impact with your company turned into a sale. You would be buried in riches beyond your wildest dreams. The difficulty arises because even nice, loyal, hardworking employees are nervous about selling, partly because out of concern for you they don't want to annoy or aggravate the customer and, as we have learned, the act of selling itself can be quite an aggravating business. People cite high-pressure selling as a reason not to sell. 'Selling things to people they don't want', 'Not taking no for an answer.' High-pressure selling is a subject in itself (and a bit of a red herring), but one example I use to help to calm worries is that I say that I have seen persuasion used where one party would not take 'no' for an answer, and they went on and on until the intended victim caved in. The strange thing is that it did no damage to the relationship at all. Perhaps it is at this point that I should explain that the person doing the persuading was six years old!

'Dad?'

'What?'

'Can I have a lolly?'

'No.'

'Go on, Dad, can I have a lolly?'

'No.'

'Why not?'

'You won't eat your lunch.'

'If I promise I'll eat my lunch, can I have a lolly?'

'No.'

'Why not?'

'Your mum would kill me.'

'Dad?

'What?'

'Mummy doesn't have to know! If I promise that I'll eat my lunch and I promise not to tell Mummy, can I have a lolly?'

'You can have a fruity one.'

'Dad?'

'What?

'I want a chocolate one!'

We were all able to do that once, but we lost it. It might seem provocative, but that stream of questions from the kid has inexorably uncovered and dealt with the hidden reasons for not doing business.

THE POINT
It may be childish but the child is clearly asking position questions to find out where it stands before the real persuading begins.

TOUCH THEIR INNER CHILD

As you will remember from the story of the child in the DIY super-store with the squashed head, we can get a long way with less able team members by getting them to imagine that they are doing business with their mothers. This may work even better with sales.

The scene. Training a gibbon to sell in an electrical store.

'Terry, your mother has come into the store and is just standing there waiting. What will you say to her?'

'Er, hello Mum.' (Cheery enough greeting, and at least he acknowledged her instead of wearing his usual threatening scowl.)

She replies 'Hello Terry,' and shuts up. There is a long embarrassing silence.

'You then say … What?'

'Er, what do you want?' (At least that's an open question.)

'I want two hundred high-output halogen bulbs.'

'What the hell do you want them for?' (Qualifying question.)

'Your dad and I are going to start a little business growing that marriageana stuff in the attic!'

'Well, you don't need halogen, you need halide, and you'll need all the special reflectors and cable.'

'That's going to cost a lot more than I expected, son.'

'Take my advice, Mum. If you want a good crop you won't regret it.'

A perfect sale. Terry loves his mum and would never rip her off, and yet he is insistent that she invests in the better quality items. He knows what she ought to have so when our team members claim that they would rather not up-sell out of respect and love for their customers, it is probably a smokescreen. They would do it for their mums, so why won't they do it for our customers? At worst they can't be bothered, but it's often shyness or discomfort at dealing with relative strangers, and they feel more comfortable dealing with people that they have a relationship with. That is why, maybe, the customer focus bit is important because it helps to start the relationship that can lead to comfortable sales.

WELL, YOU HIRED THE IDIOT

If we could take a moment out here, this part of the chapter is dedicated to getting your non-sales and less able people selling for you. The benefits are huge but just consider why you are employing less able people. If you sell a prestige product, I am sure you would agree it helps to sell it from a prestige premises for which you would be happy to pay a premium. If you manufactured beautiful jewellery you might be prepared to pay hundreds of pounds a square foot for the best address in Bond Street – a world renowned place for the sale of jewels, but you would only pay a few pounds a foot for a pitch in the suburbs. Why? There must be a clear benefit for paying those exorbitant rentals. It must be because you think that the prestige address will do a better job of selling for you. You cheerfully accept that paying hundreds of pounds a square foot can be added on to your expenses because the expected earnings will handsomely compensate you, yet when it comes to people, there isn't too much difference in their hourly rate, whatever your market or marketplace. Admittedly there is some, but a shop worker in the West End of London doesn't earn ten or twenty times the average, where the rents can achieve this. Possibly, just possibly, premium people could generate premium returns.

THE LAZY BRAND

This is of course the simple basics of sales that everyone can master, but true skilful selling is like a martial art with nuances and finesse, delicate touches and profound subtleties that will seduce and woo the target into ever greater investment that delights and satisfies them, and handsomely profits the practitioner. It seems however that the world has given up on this delicate art and has instead developed dumb, shabby products for dumb, shabby people to sell. This leaves us with a stunning opportunity. Take new houses as an example. In the same area with the same location why is one house more expensive? Answer – because it is bigger. Imagine if there were two houses on identical plots of identical size, and apparently of similar design, but one was as much as 50 per cent dearer, many thousands of pounds more. Would you buy it? Before you answer that, just think, would you pay more for a nice little Porsche, or a big Ford? I hope the choice is obvious but the reason may not be. Perhaps you are an automotive whiz-kid who can see the difference in build and component quality, but more than likely it's the reputation of the two manufacturers that colours your choice. That reputation, or should we say hype, has currently been whittled down to be expressed as branding. The big companies have become lazy and complacent and have simply let the cult of the brand do their selling for them. Just because it has Sony, Rolex, Mercedes, or IBM on it, they assume we don't now need to know how it was constructed: 'You can trust the brand!'

There is even a danger of a temptation to bank on the reputation of your brand, and reduce the quality of the components to increase profits. What this has produced is that retailing can be reduced to filling a huge unattractive shed with branded products and staffing it with semi-literate chimps, who just have to prevent us stealing things and take our money to fulfil their role. The brand does the rest of the work.

THOUGHT

It is dangerous to let the brand do our selling.

If you had great salespeople, they could sell anything at any price. In other words, they could create a mini brand on the spot just with their technique.

BEWARE THE BRAND

As we saw in our global bit, if you have secured a brand, you can have production sited anywhere – the cheaper the better. The dangers for us are that we may work in production for a brand, and prove a little too expensive for our masters. We may own a brand that has gone out of fashion. Brand awareness is great as long as the punters don't wake up and decide that our products are naff. Levi, Ray Ban, Rolex, to name but a few: all are in danger of being identified with a certain type of consumer – possibly a 'sad' one. Thirdly, maybe we have a business that doesn't own a famous brand. The answer to our problem is … Selling. One wonders if there is a chicken and egg situation here. Did the brands grow when selling became crap, or did selling become crap when the brands grew?

Not to bore you with too much historical detail, but fifty years ago when you went to buy something, you would visit a supplier or manufacturer who would regale you with the features and benefits of his offering. The Holy Grail was to find one USP, or unique selling point. Apparently when you realised how their product would uniquely solve your current problem, you would be putty in their hands. There was a technique that referred to FBI – Features, Benefits or Incentives – and I am sure that you are yawning at just the thought of raking through these mouldy old dog turds of long-buried sales methods. Well so am I, but just like the 'smiling' bit with customers, I am astonished to find even the simplest stuff has just been lost or ignored, so pardon me but let's raise FBI from its grave for a moment. F stood for feature. This cutlery is stainless steel, these brakes are ABS. The argument was that these were simple statements of fact that had no pay-off or 'what's in it for me' for the customer. Sales people were taught to state a feature and then say 'Which means that…' and this would then provoke the benefit. 'These forks are stainless steel which means that they never rust, stain or tarnish', but then it was felt that this still might not induce the customer to buy unless there was an incentive, or unless a person gained from that benefit. So salespeople were encouraged to add 'and that means for you ...' 'These brakes are ABS, which means that the car cannot skid, and that means for you the peace of mind that your family are much safer travelling in this vehicle.' Obvious and simple, I know, but it does require a proportion of product knowledge and interpretation, and application of that knowledge. It also requires gentle but probing interpersonal skills that impart the customer with the vital information that can tie them specifically to the product. These are all skills that are way beyond your average superstore chimp, but it never became a real problem because branding came along to mask the loss of retail skills. 'What's this washing machine like?' 'It's a Zanussi.' 'What can it do?' 'We sell loads of them.' 'Is it any good?' 'Don't get many back.' Bigger brand, bigger price, safer buy.

Then computers came along. They started off with brands like IBM, ICL and the like. They also got those premium prices. Then some clever sod discovered that the actual mechanics of the things were modular and could be built for a fraction of the cost that the big boys charged, but how to market against the names? The IBM clone was born. Of course, IBM went apeshit and I believe quite a few writs flew about, but they lost the battle. The punters meanwhile learned that the cheap clones performed more or less as well as their dearer prototypes. Now, because the public were not being controlled or led by intelligent sales, people were led simply by price and a new element, specification. The outcome is a spec sheet with mega, giga, terra huge numbers, and a beige box full of cheap crappy Far Eastern components. The software that makes the thing work in the meantime is brand dominated, with the mighty Microsoft ruling the world so comprehensively that almost no one even questions it. The problem arises for the computer giants when the consumers who have been led higher and higher in the specification race suddenly wake up and realise that the capacity of the computer is beyond their possible requirements on capacity. It must be near the time where everyone has a computer and many have had one for two or three years. I have a four year old machine that was, in its day, state of the art and very expensive. In specification it is far behind and is on paper worthless, but it does what we bought it for and meets every demand I make of it. I even prefer its older but simpler and more reliable operating system. Sure, when it busts or can't do what I want, I will change it. It's a bit like a washing machine. I bet when they came out they cost thousands and only the rich or technical freaks had one. Then they became affordable and every home wanted one. In two or three years, ten million or so machines would be required but then demand would decline to the replacement market. This would not encourage 'Washingmachineseller' or 'Washing Machine World' to spring up in warehouses around every town. Ask yourself, did you need that GIGABITE? Then the writing is on the wall for those who don't think they need to sell.

THOUGHT

We have become trapped by brand and specification. 'This is an Intel powered two gig IBM laptop for two hundred quid less than the shop next door.' Then we make so little money, we can't afford desire-building staff. A good salesperson can conjure demand out of thin air. It was called creative selling and it may be the way out of the trap.

SELL THE DIFFERENCE

Let us return to our apparently overpriced house. If the difference in the price was caused not by the size, but by the quality of the materials, someone would have to sell the benefits of that quality. We live in a truly complex world where just coping with our own complications is hard enough without coping with all the peripheral stuff that clutters our lives. Things used to be so much simpler. When I was a kid, I built my own TV set. A magazine called Wireless World ran a series of simple articles and within a few weeks I had a working TV. Recently I bought a new TV and it came with a book the size of a telephone directory on the workings of the remote control. I simply don't understand it. I am sure it does things that would increase my viewing pleasure enormously, but I don't have the foggiest idea what those things are. Lurking in my utility room I had a new washing machine, supposedly the best in the world. I couldn't work it, I wished I hadn't bought it, I wanted my simple old one with a single knob on the front that would grind away for an hour or two and tear the arse out of my pants. The world is oh so very complicated and frightening that I need a friend, a knowledgeable friend who I can trust. A friend who can guide me to the correct buying decisions. NOT the chimp in the big shed. We will, for the sake of clarity, create a temporary mythical figure who will contain all the virtues the chimp lacks. He will function in any situation, be it service engineer, retailer, van driver or storeman. Maybe he won't be the suited and booted sales rep or manager, but that's the beauty of this paragon – he outperforms the apparent professional salesperson every time, for reasons that will be explained.

THE PARAGON

So let's meet him. He is older, has greying hair, is perhaps wearing a carpenter's apron or dust coat, he has half moon glasses and a soft rural accent. We want to see him perform in our new house, but first let us see how he sold me the television. As mentioned, television technology has become very complicated, but after fifteen years of watching the same TV, I felt it was time for a new one. The truth is that I had wanted a new one for about ten years, but every time I thought I had grasped the advancement I wanted, everything would change. First it was FST (flat screen technology), then stereo. I would go in to a store with my tatty bit of paper.

'I want an FST TV with stereo.'

'That's old hat, we are waiting for Dolby pro logic.'

Later:

'I want an FST TV with Dolby pro logic home cinema.'

'It's all going to be wide screen.'

Later:

'I want a wide screen, pro logic, home cinema.'

'You do know they are all going digital?'

I read 'What Telly' magazine and now I think I've got it taped. I want a digital, wide screen TV, with separate DVD and cinema sound with 100 Hz scan.

Armed with this, I set off for my local electrical superstore. I saw the set I thought I wanted and at a very competitive price. Actually, a bit too competitive. I found a little chap who was contentedly scratching his bottom and sporting a badge which read 'Terry, Audio visual consultant, how may I help?'

'Terry, my fine young chum, if you would leave your posterior alone for just a moment, I would like to trouble you with a question.'

'Uh?' came the rapier repost.

'This TV seems very reasonably priced, is it 100 Hz?'

'Yep.'

'Are you sure?'

'Um ...'

I started to feel uneasy – a new discordant note had been added to Terry's symphony of vacant and gormless indifference. That note was just a hint of panic. He shifted uneasily.

'You don't know, do you? The truth is you don't even know what 100Hz is, do you?'

The confession was grudging. 'So?'

'So, does anybody here know?'

'I'll fetch me manager.' With that he put his hands tight to his side, fists clenched and started to yell, giving me the impression that his head was turning a full 360 degrees as he did so. 'Bob! Bob! Bob!'

The badge read 'Robert, Audio visual manager. How may I help?'

'Is there a problem, Terry?' he snarled.

'Yes', I interjected, 'Terry doesn't know whether this TV is 100 Hz or not. Do you?'

'Yep.'

'Well, is it?'

'Yep.' There was an almost undetectable tremor in the 'yep' and that same shuffling unease.

'Ha-ha! You don't know either, do you?'

'So?'

'Does anyone know? Would Head Office know?'

'Doubt it. They just send this stuff in boxes. We don't get the same stock from one week to the next, but it is cheap.'

Cheap. That is the key to this – fast and cheap. Without sales, products have to be fast and cheap. Without sales, everything is shoddy, plastic, short-lived, and disappointing. With sales?

As we drove away from the out of town shopping experience, I saw a small shop. The sign read 'Perry Perkins TV'. We stopped and went in. A tinkly bell on a spring heralded our entrance. He appeared, the halo of white hair, the half round glasses, the overall and the rural accent.

''Ello sir, 'ello madam, lovely to see you.' His eyes twinkled.

'Stab me vitals,' I thought, 'he actually means it.'

'What can I do for you, me lovers?'

'I want a new telly, I want Dolby pro log …'

'Whoa, whoa,' he cried, holding up his palm. 'Hold your horses. Let me just ask you what do you really love watching?'

'Films, movies.'

'Do you like to watch sport, sir?'

'Not much, actually.'

'Well, if it's cinema you're after, let me introduce you to the Panasonic, wide screen, now you've got your 100 Hz quitric tube in this one, that means a flicker free picture, which for you sir means glorious Technicolor that's sharper than the cinema itself. A set, sir, that will bring you endless pleasure.'

(I've just been FBI-ed)

'What about the Sony?'

'A lovely set, sir, but can't touch the Panasonic when it comes to movies.'

'Mm, very expensive, isn't it?'

'Just forget the price for a moment, it won't be a problem. I'll just put on a DVD and you see if it really is the set you would like.'

Of course it was. The price wasn't a problem because when I saw the TV was the one I wanted, I would have paid any price. Although gentle and helpful, he used some classic old sales techniques. When I came in with demands, he stopped that and took control, not letting the customer conduct the sale. He asked questions, he didn't conduct a demonstration until he had qualified the customer and identified the needs. He tied the features, the benefits, and the incentives in beautifully and then elegantly set aside my price objections. Old, basic chestnuts, I know, but it is dangerous to abandon them particularly when you see the fascinating implication of applying our paragon to that expensive house.

AROUND THE HOUSES

We walk into the show home.

'Oh hello again, sir and madam, it's lovely to see you. What would you like me to show you?'

'Well we wondered why this house is so much dearer than the one next door.'

'Bless you for askin', sir. Take a look at these floors, sir, solid oak they are sir, and the door, all mahogany on hardwood frames. Sir, your great-grandchildren will still be swinging on those doors and no harm will come to them.'

Hardwood frames, oak floors? No chance. Maybe in a flash city flat we would bung in a few Neff or Mielle appliances to give a bit of glitz but we are back to branding. But I tell you, I *would* like a house that had no cardboard walls, that had solid wood doors. No builder dares to build it.

'Do you know how much that would cost?'

The reason is tragically simple. They do not employ anyone who is capable of selling that level of quality. Therefore this means that the competence and ability of your selling function will influence your production decisions. If you don't want to splosh around in the turgid swamps of crap products made to the tightest prices, either become a globally famous brand, or teach all your people to sell.

THE POINT

You can only purchase or manufacture prestige products at premium prices if you are confident that you have the people who are skilful enough to sell them. Selling ability = price premium.

I don't want to disappoint you with simple stuff, I want to wow you with the cutting-edge guru stuff, but if what you make is governed by what you can sell, this might be simple territory but it is very important. Let's take the proposition to its most ludicrously simple level. 'Well then, are you going to buy it?' Very crude, very simple, but when was the last time anyone in your enterprise said that or anything like that to a customer? When we meet the outside world at any point of contact we must intend to sell to it.

EXPLODING ORANGES

Near me is a greengrocer of the most traditional sort. Small and tatty with roller shutters instead of windows. I could not believe that anyone could make a living from such a place. One night I saw the old chap who owned the place, locking up for the night. His trembly old woolly gloved hands shook as he turned the key in the icy padlock. 'Poor old fellow,' I thought as I saw him shuffling painfully across the pavement to his turbo-powered Bentley, in which he roared home. How does he do that? He obviously makes a fortune, but how? The answer is that he has a genetic propensity to sell. He intends to sell. He loves his customers, he's kind to his customers, but he intends to sell to them.

If I entered your greengrocery store and asked how much your cauliflowers were, your answer might well be '98p'. I would say 'then I'll have one'. What have you just sold me? Answer, nothing. You didn't sell me anything. On ledgers we write 'Sales' but I wonder how many of those are sales? Perhaps they would be more accurate if we wrote 'Stuff people have bought from us'. At the best, all the customer care/relationship stuff simply prevents our teams from obstructing the process of people buying stuff from us.

Try buying a cauliflower from our above mentioned greengrocer. He greets us with a huge cheery smile.

'Hello, me lovers, what can I do for you today?'

'One of your cauliflowers, please, Mr Smiggins.'

'There you are then, me dears, lovely firm hearted beauty. Tell me, were you going to eat this one tonight?'

'I was. Why?'

'I'll tell you why I asked, I've just had the Jersey potatoes in, lovely waxy ones, all packed in soft peat. Peels theirselves they do, couple of pounds of them with that cauli – 'ave yourself a banquet, so you will.'

'Sounds lovely. OK.'

'There you are then. It's getting a bit chilly, ain't it? Trouble with this cold weather is that it gets on the kiddies' chests. Children suffer when its cold. Actually its funny that we were talking about your children, 'cause I was in the van with Charlie when there was this whacking great bang from the back. "What was that?" I asked him. "Its them oranges you bought, Mr Smiggins. They're so packed with vitamin C, they're exploding so they are." Now, with half a dozen of them, it'll set them kids of yours up a treat. Now let me see, you've had your cauli, the spuds, and the oranges – that'll be four pounds and a penny – call it four pounds for cash. Lovely to have seen you, see you again soon.' With that he turns to the next customer.

'Now sir, what can I do for you?' but suddenly a look of panic spreads across his face and he turns back to you.

'Oh, what's the matter with me, I'd forget me head if it wasn't screwed on. I forgot to tell you, I've got the Christmas satsumas coming in, and I knows how you love 'em, so I'm going to put some aside for you, special. Lovely and juicy they are, come in and ask for me next week and I'll have put some aside for you.'

He has just tripled his turnover, he has just made that next appointment for the next selling session. A simple man using simple methods, but he has just sold three times as much as we could. The theme of this book (if there is one) seems to gel into the basic concept that everyone is involved from arming the peasant, to the process, to the customer focus, yet when it comes to sales, we tend to once again leave it to the sales department. I have just waded laboriously through the latest cerebral sales book. Advanced is not the word for it, so much psychobabble, impossible-to-read graphs, tables and bollocks. Maybe if I were mega-generous, it may work for the cutting edge, working at the highest level, big ticket writers, but for ordinary people? No chance. If every single person involved in your enterprise learned simple selling skills, however basic, and applied those skills, you would be beating cash-waving customers off with a stick. You would not have time to count your cash, you would just have to weigh it in sacks.

THE POINT

The simplest most basic sales techniques applied by all your people to every customer could triple your turnover instantly.

THE ONLY GOOD PIG

Every time you go into a coffee shop or cafeteria, and you ask for a coffee, you get a coffee. You might, but only might, be asked, 'Anything else?' but what if they sold you a slice of their delicious home-made cake?

'Try a slice of our delicious home-made cake.'

'Better not, I'm on a diet.'

'Go on, spoil yourself – look at it, its as light as air. Have a taste, isn't that the best you've ever tasted?'

This is where you collapse in despair because your part-time counter assistant is still working on the secret of fire and the control of simple bodily functions, and your cake is a weighty factory-built horror. No one said this was easy. It's about Yin and Yang, horrid staff and crap products, which results in no customers. Every sales book we read fails to address that. Clever techniques, ripping japes and wheezes, will not save you if your offering stinks. Be brutal, is the cake the best you have ever tasted, is the staff member chirpy, enthusiastic and ready to go for it? Go and get that right, now. Done it? Great, because now you can increase the quality and PRICE of your offering because your people are going to promote it.

Does this constitute pushiness or conflict with our dedication to customer care? I don't think so. Why take care of something that is of no benefit to you? This was neatly summed up when I met a farmer leaning on a gate. He greeted me with a cheery wave and, as we passed the time of day, a large pig came and nuzzled up to him. Its snout tried to penetrate the dark secrets of his capacious pockets.

'Hello old girl,' he said, patting the creature on the head and scratching its ears. The pig, giving grunts of contentment, rubbed against him. 'You're looking for an apple, aren't you girl? Now let's see if I've got one.' The farmer made a big performance of playfully searching in every pocket while the pig looked on in anticipation. Sure enough he produced a huge red fruit which the pig munched in ecstasy. While still scratching the joyful animal's ear, the farmer turned to me. 'This is Rosy, this is, a lovely beast. Loves her apples, she do. She's going off to be bacon next week, aren't you girl?' The poor creature appeared to nod enthusiastically.

I was stunned. 'You mean you're going to kill it?'

'I'm a pig farmer, what do you think I do with pigs? They're not pets, this is how I make my living.'

'But how can you be so nice to her?'

'Because pigs thrive on kindness. A happy pig makes good meat. Why? Do you think I should be cruel?'

A brutal truth, but of course he was right. The factory-bred pigs that are kept in the dark, have their teeth removed to prevent fighting and are fed bits of each other make pale, spudgy, unappetising meat. Now isn't that just like customers? The ones that are herded and crowded into big sheds, treated cruelly and with indifference, produce a rotten crop. Yet if you cuddle, love and take gentle rewarding care of your customers, they will thrive – but there's little point in doing it if you fail to profit from them. You just end up with a yard full of pet pigs. The way to harvest your rich crop of customers is to sell to them, and everybody who works for you should intend to sell to them.

THOUGHT

Our customer care must be faultless of course, but don't forget why you are doing it. You are fattening your customers to profit from them, and selling is the method of harvest.

THE SELLING TORNADO

We need to start by considering some very simple and basic selling skills. Again, we are faced by the dichotomy between the high-falutin stuff that goes on in sales seminars, and what is actually happening on the ground. When one is faced with a room full of hardened sales pros, and when reviewing the basics such as asking questions or selling the benefits, a huge, bored sigh of 'we've done it, seen it, heard it all before' goes up. To survive in the guru business you have to gee whiz such audiences with the latest and most sophisticated manipulation techniques. The latest books on sales are actually not only incomprehensible, but are in effect 500 page advertising leaflets for some eye-wateringly expensive consultancy training programme. T.O.R.N.A.D.O. Touch, Orientated, Reordering, Non-committal, Attention, Desire, Observations (I just made all that up before you become tempted to send me money to get your team on the Tornado programme). My only reservation, apart perhaps from the fact that I'm too stupid to understand them, is that they don't work. Perhaps your company has just undertaken such a programme, did sales go up because of it? Didn't think so. If you found that comment too provocative, then ask yourself when was the last time that an uninvited salesperson sat across the desk from you, whereupon you became strangely dizzy and placed an enormous order with them? (Well, not one that you didn't subsequently cancel, anyway.)

THINK ABOUT

You send your salespeople on ever more sophisticated programmes because they whinge about how basic the last one was. But they are not even applying the basics. Send them on a Formula One racing course before they know what the ignition key is for? I don't think so.

DON'T EXPECT THEM TO SELL

Perhaps we should take a completely different view of our sales process. Perhaps our salespeople shouldn't be doing our selling. Maybe we misuse them. For years one of the names given to sales-people, particularly in industry, has been 'rep'. That is short for 'representative'. That doesn't suggest anything about selling. It suggests representation. I think the thread in all of this that I have just noticed, is that one of the failures of modern business is that traffic is all one way. Web sites are just computerised catalogues, they don't ask us what we would like; CRM is just bored people manning a database. Why don't they ring us first before we have a problem? Reps are sent out to sell the output of production.

Now consider this, we make stainless steel thingies. Our sales team have had a stonking year and have sold 5000 thingies. Classically, what we would do is sit down and plan our campaign for next year. Our tough talking, firm but fair sales director (don't you just hate people like that?) decides that it would be a good idea to stretch the team just a little, by upping their targets. Maybe just ten per cent to 5500 thingies. Reams of old bollocks is spout-ed about targets and goal setting. Should targets be achievable? Should they be just out of reach, to stretch people? Why don't we ask the salesforce how much they can sell? Actually that doesn't work either because the poor saps are just as brainwashed, and they set themselves unachievable targets in a pathetic attempt to impress. Don't send them out just to sell, but use them as, dare I suggest it, 'representatives', problem solvers, ambassadors, and most important of all, gatherers of information. Can I suggest that production doesn't tell them how many to sell, they tell production how many to make?

'Make 3000 thingies.'

'But you sold 5000 last year.'

'Yep, now everybody's got one, we need to promote our plastic ones, and I reckon we'll need 7000 of those.'

We should use them as our early warning system, otherwise it would be like a general climbing from his bunker, seeing his city bombed flat and saying 'Hmmm, I think I'd better speak to Radar about this.'

If you look at departments in a company, they have become obsessed and dominated by their titles, believing that their name gives them total dominance and ownership of their discipline. Accounts control the money, but they must understand that they don't make that money and should do nothing to obstruct the money-making process. Production, however clever, should only produce what can be sold. Sales should only oversee the sales process and should actively encourage all the other departments to indulge in a bit of selling. In other words, all the departments should be masters and instructors of their core discipline, and their task is to help everyone else to take a share of the activity. A successful self-employed sole trader is a good role model, because they contain all this activity in one body. They wouldn't win themselves a nice new client and then send them a threatening letter for the payment of the deposit. All the functions are in one head, unless the person is barking mad, and there is total communication with no buck-passing.

If everyone sells, instead of having a 500-employee company with ten in sales, you will have a 500-salespeople company with ten experts organising and directing the sales effort.

POINT

The sales department may be the master of the sale process but they shouldn't be the only ones doing it.

IT'S WHAT THEY KNOW

If you looked at a retail group twenty years ago, virtually every shop-based member of staff was referred to as a salesperson. That is what they were, they sold things to people. If you bought the shoes, they were taught to 'accessorise' – in other words, you got the belt, the handbag and the hat. Slowly they started to be described as 'consultants' or 'assistants'. In some electrical stores you may still get an abrasive little turd, who gets right up your nose with some intrusive overpriced warranty that makes no financial sense but, apart from that, no one sells anymore. Why? Maybe it is because school children are so completely useless at social interaction that simply preventing them from being sullen, aggressive or even abusive is the best you can expect. Perhaps because there is a feeling that if you fill a huge shed with cheap crap, it will sell itself.

If you look at the TV advertisements, even in their airy-fairy, fantasy world of happy shoppers, the best they offer is friendly staff, not knowledgeable sales staff who can guide you to happy decisions. Just grinning half-wits that smile or wave happily at you as you wade around their depressing world of shoddy rubbish.

Is it going to be chicken or egg? Do we start producing fine, top price, value-added goods, and then train our team to sell them, or do we produce a selling team that would be wasted unless they have the top value stuff to sell? You see, the two are inextricably linked. Bad staff can't sell quality items, bad product isn't worth selling.

Laziness on the part of companies may be part of the reason. In my television story, it is clear that the first stumbling block was product knowledge. Basic and boring, I know, but go into a supplier, trade counter or shop, point at an expensive item and say 'Why should I buy the dearer one?' They will not be able to tell you. If you employ people like that, you are wasting your time. They must know why, they must become the customers' professional partner, guiding them and knowledgeably advising them to buy the best.

This may be a distant dream, but some simple selling skills would certainly go a long way. In the next section we will explore selling skills – hopefully up to a fairly sophisticated level, but first we will look at the simple ones that anyone can and should use.

- *Intend to sell.*
- *Get back to basics.*
- *Use questions to find your true position.*
- *Everyone can and should be selling.*
- *The value of your offer is tied to your team's ability to sell it.*
- *Premium products require premium sales.*
- *Branding is the lazy way out.*
- *Don't bother taking care of the customer if you don't intend to profit from them.*
- *Don't expect profits from customers you don't take care of.*
- *Sell more, then sell even more.*
- *Sales should be used to oversee and encourage the sales function in everyone else.*

THE POWER OF PERSUASION 6

If we are going to start slow and build up to a crescendo of frenzied flogging, the most basic selling skill to consider is simply asking someone to buy. You may wonder what happens to gurus and change agents during their lean times and the explanation may be found in their CVs. They will always claim to have an encyclopaedic knowledge of change.

This is because prior to strutting about pontificating for huge fees, you would have found them sitting in the street on an old sleeping bag, accompanied by a flea-bitten dog. Their cry is plaintive and reasonably successful. 'Spare any change, please' – hence the knowledge of change.

Surprisingly, people give them money. No explanation, no benefit offered, just 'Give me money.' They don't say they're staving, unemployed or ill. They say 'Give me money.' The weird thing is, we do. Not all of us, of course, but enough to make a tidy living until the next consultancy project comes along. If we can get money for nothing, then it would be a wheeze if we did have something to offer. I think that any business can imagine the financial transformation if all their employees with any kind of customer contact simply asked people to buy.

A waitress serves you coffee and says 'Would you like a cake with that?' The meter reader says 'Would you like our five star service contract?' The receptionist asks 'Have you ever thought of owning a 170,000 ton bulk carrier?' Of course, not everyone buys (particularly not bulk carriers), but in the early days of brutal, gritty sales, one of the key motivators was the knowledge that it was a numbers game. Even the most incompetent of salespeople with the naffest product could sell to, say, one in every hundred of the people they had leapt out on. The instant answer then would be to jump out on more people. All you have to do now, this instant, is to get everyone who is involved in your enterprise to become sales aware.

THINK ABOUT THIS

Put on your very best clothes, go up to people in the street and in your best accent say, 'Look, I'm terribly sorry to bother you, and this is so embarrassing, but I wonder if you could spare me £5?' You will make a fortune. Get other people into smart clothes, get them to do it and keep £3 for themselves, and give you £2. You now have a company.

- Small business (the hairy dog bloke) is often held back by a lack of slick presentation.
- The first step is to get everyone who works for you to ask for business.
- People should cost you less than they bring in (they must all bring in something).

BUT CAN THEY DO IT?

Before we get really started, I suppose I ought to mention a disturbing report I have just read that suggests that 60 per cent or more of staff are disaffected. They apparently will do just enough to avoid getting fired, and no more. That, I suppose, would be the condensed essence of this book: how to get all your people doing good things for your business. You may have wondered, with all the wonderful management books about, why commerce is almost universally crap. Perhaps that bored voice on the phone, the arse-scratching waiter or the cheerily abusive service engineer have all been trained in customer care or sales, they just defiantly resist ever applying these techniques. Don't be smug, you know it's your fault. Forget motivation and encouragement for a moment, important though they are, and consider how much importance you are putting on selling. If you caught a member of your team stealing cash you would fire them on the spot, but pissing off customers is tolerated with a resigned shrug. Failing to sell to them barely even raises a glimmer. Selling things to your customers is the most important thing that you do. With no extra investment or training, just getting your team to ask 'Do you want one?' would add a minimum of 5–10 per cent to the top line. With some complicated maths, which to be frank I don't understand, I have seen a statistician show how 10 per cent on the top line with no increase in overheads can result in a 100 per cent increase in profit. Search me how they work that one out but, rest assured, whatever it is, it is worth having. Here endeth the lesson. Let's cut to the chase. We have covered 'Will you buy one?' as a technique. Simple and elegant it may be, but there is a small drawback and that is that the intended victim may say 'no'. This has taxed the minds of sales gurus for years, and their solution is sophisticated and clear, and breathtakingly stupid. It works on the cheery principle that if a customer tends to say 'no', which is undesirable, then ask a question that the answer cannot be 'no' to. 'Do you want it?' becomes 'Where do you want it?' and 'Can I help you?' becomes 'How can I help you?' I have seen an auditorium filled with 3000 baying salespeople all chanting after the white-suited paragon 'NEVER ASK A SAY NO QUESTION!'

The police have taken this on with a semi-religious fervour, and now, instead of interrogating with a good old piece of rubber hose or an accidental fall down the cell steps, are disciples of open questioning. Although the burly police officer is manly and tough, by becoming cuddly and empathising and using those open questions he can gently open the recidivist's callous shell. Dream on.

WE ASK ALL THE QUESTIONS

Questions do give power and at a higher level, different sorts of questions can have different effects, but for now, let's just start with simple questions which still have enough power to give a startling increase in revenue. For this experiment, take our least able member of staff. Currently, when approached by a potential customer face to face or by phone, the response to requests is 'nope' or 'yep'.

To be fair, we ourselves, although a lot more polite, tend to answer 'yes' or 'no' to questions. If we can learn to avoid doing this and answer a question with a question, things move forward dramatically. I have turned this answering a question with a question thing into quite a habit, to the point that a friend asked me the other day 'Geoff, why do you always answer a question with a question?'

My reply was, 'Do I?'

In the quest for customer care companies have had little trouble creating responses like: 'I'm Brian, your waiter for this evening', or 'Thank you for visiting Enemas'. Therefore as long as it's simple, we should have no problem with a basic sales routine. Say you own a furniture shop, the phone rings and one of your Saturday part-timers picks up the phone.

'ThankyouforringingSofaLandI'mTracey'owmayIhelpyou?'

'Oh yes, have you still got those red three-piece suites that you had at half price?'

The answer is either 'Yep' or 'Nope'.

Now, surprisingly, the answer is always the same. 'Oh thank you so much, goodbye.'

What we don't know is exactly why the person rang. Actually we know bugger all about them. Who they are, where they are, what they wanted, and how much they wanted to spend. Machiavelli said 'knowledge is power'. If we look into the vacant eyes and see the slack jaw of our least talented team members, we would be inclined to suggest that they have little knowledge and therefore it stands to reason they have little power – but then they are not seekers of knowledge. A seeker of knowledge has to ask questions. Doesn't it drive you nuts when you get back to the office to be greeted by 'Someone rang when you was out'?

'Who was it?'

'They never said.'

'Where did they ring from?'

'They never said.'

'What did they want?'

'They never said that, neither.'

'Did they say anything or give any clue that might be of use?'

'They was furious.'

Let's make them seekers of knowledge, ban 'yes' or 'no'. Make everyone speak only the language of questions, and riches will rain upon you from the sky. Back to the furniture shop.

'Have you still got those red three-piece suites that you had at half price?'

'I'm not sure, was the red one the one you particularly wanted?'

'Yes.'

Now, even though we can see hundreds of them from where we are standing, we don't say 'that's OK, we've got stacks of them'. Although that sounds helpful, and maybe is helpful, it loosens our control of the customer, but more of that later. What we do say is 'I'm not sure that we have still got some. I will just go and check. May I ask who is calling, please?' We teach people to remain silent until there is a reply.

'Cyril Jenkins.'

'Do you have a number there, Mr Jenkins?'

'01446589.'

'Thank you so much. If we do still have one, would you like me to put it on one side for you?'

'Yes please.'

A bit of off-stage shuffling, then a slightly breathless 'We have got one, and I have put it away for you. When can we expect you?'

I won't go into all the gory details, but you may see that this is a distinct improvement on 'nope' or 'yep'. Distinct improvement is a giant leap forward. The drum-beating sales book of the past would trumpet this sort of thing as 'never fail'. I would like to be a bit more modest and say 'sometimes works'.

Maybe your reception or stores receive a hundred or so phone calls per day. If just two or three are turned into sales, that could be 500 to 750 new sales a year. I don't know what your average order value is, but I bet an extra 500 or so wouldn't go amiss. Even the service engineer who perhaps has only 1000 customer contacts a year would achieve 30 new sales at those modest percentages.

To return to the on-going saga of my new washing machine. Our trendy new computer-controlled wonder had developed an anxiety-related complaint – to wit on the sight of my pants, it wouldn't open the door. When, after a period of Gestalt-based counselling, it was persuaded that washing them was fulfilling its role and was in fact reaffirming its validity, it then refused to relinquish said pants. The engineer came and said that we had a right to reject the machine (to be fair, it was able to cope with rejection surprisingly well, as it left only six inches of standing water in my kitchen as a testimony to its angst). We asked him what he recommended, he sighed wistfully and his eyes rose to Heaven. The expression can only be likened to the Victorian prints of St Joan, moments before martyrdom. I think it's called rapture. He told us of a German machine and how he had struggled to raise the money to own it, and after having to sell a kidney and one of his children, he had become the proud possessor of one. This guy was a washing machine enthusiast. He told us that although this machine was heavy and ugly, inside was an engineering miracle.

Three times the cost of its nearest rival, it was the summit of washing machine design. Of course we bought one. I howled at the bill and when a thing that looked like a panzer tank arrived, I must say I did not share our chum's ecstasy, but he was right. It looks like a panzer tank because it's built like a panzer tank. When my pants need a jolly good seeing to, they get it, but at other times they are caressed and massaged in a cloud of gentle suds. The thing is a miracle. I would not have bought one in a showroom, it looks dreadful. The engineer sold it to me. It's a shame he works for the competition.

THOUGHT

There is no reason that you should not expect everyone who works with you to use simple questions to gain information and conduct basic sales.

AND THIS IS HOW IT IS DONE

There you have it, a simple sale for ordinary people who up until now do not see their role as in sales. It pays such huge dividends that it would do us no harm to do a little dismantling to understand why it is gob-smackingly profitable.

Firstly, let us examine the power of questions. Not the old guff about open or closed, but just the simple power of questions. The main and simple reason for asking someone a question is to get information. This may seem blindingly obvious, but most salespeople spend their time giving away information. In computer sales places the sales staff seem to fall into two major camps, namely the surly monosyllabic chimps or the spotty, geeky, propeller heads with verbal diarrhoea. We have dealt at some length with the first, so let's examine the second type. He witters on about bytes, ROMs, bands, ethernets, WHAT? Machiavelli said 'knowledge is power', but this one is giving away knowledge, not gaining knowledge. Therefore power is being given away, not gained.

One of the great misunderstandings of sales is that what is required is the 'gift of the gab'. Nothing could actually be further from the truth, and in a previous book, I called the skill of persuasive selling not the 'gift of the gab', but the 'gift of the earhole'! Every writer on sales, me included, has accused over-enthusiastic salespeople of talking too much. There's a little reminder that says things like, 'we were born with two ears and one mouth', to remind us of the ratio of listening to talking when it comes to sales. Actually, if mother nature had intended that, we would have about forty ears. This is all true but I feel distinctly uneasy as I write this. In my early days of guru-ing, it wouldn't be unusual for a company to gather together a small herd of ultra-keen recruits from its sales department and inflict me on them for a bit of sales training. Their enthusiasm would lead them to cock up demonstrations, appointments and sales. They did talk too much, they did fail to gain information, and they didn't listen, but what we are trying to do here is to get our non-sales people selling. There is a subtle difference, and that is that a great number of them couldn't give a toss. Strangely enough, and quite falsely, you would be led by the classic criteria to believe they are the perfect salespeople, inasmuch as the potential customer is at best met by monosyllables or worse a strong silence. Before the

FACT

We all need to sell

poor old peasants cop too much of the blame, I would say that this runs from top to bottom of the company. If we aren't in sales, we don't sell.

We recently changed accountants. Why? Because a senior partner of a major accountancy firm rang and sold his company's services. Most professional partners would believe these sort of antics to be beneath them. In fact I believe that a lot of professional associations even banned self-promotion until recently.

THE FARTING CAT

Let me say it again. Whenever I bump into anyone from your company, from the board members to the tea lady, they should cheerfully and enthusiastically promote the products and services that provide their incomes. If your enterprise does not exhibit that behaviour, you are losing out. In ordinary front line staff these skills have been neglected to the point that they are almost beyond redemption. In a previous book I mentioned the farting cat and the talking bottom. It would do no harm to reprise them here. As we have seen, remaining silent is a great sales technique. There was a great fashion for people at sales conferences to shout 'Shut up and Sell!' but that mechanic, the stores man, the shop girl have shut up and they don't make me want to buy anything. In truth they make me want to rush at them with a big stick. So where is it going wrong?

I had this huge, fat, squashy ginger cat, and if he wasn't watched like a hawk when the bin bag was removed from the bin, he would dive in to get at that horrible festering swamp that lives at the bottom of bins. The rotting food wastes that had turned to a sort of pungent, mucusy, living jelly were his favourite delectables. He would eat them with enthusiasm until chased off. After one of these special snacks, he would stroll into the living room and settle against the radiator. Rolling partially on to this back, he became virtually boneless with relaxation. At this point this huge ball of soft, relaxed fur would begin to fart. At first the occupants of the room would look accusingly at each other until the slumbering culprit was found contentedly dreaming beautiful dreams, while noxious efluviants were emitted to the gentle bubblings and hissings of escaping gas. Now if you observed the same cat crouched in the garden watching the small birds failing their first flying lessons, you would see a very different creature. Every muscle tense and rippling, eyes wide, lips flexing in anticipation. The whole thing like a coiled spring ready to explode forward on its prey. If I showed you a photograph of the flatulent personality and asked you what it was, you would say that it was a cat doing nothing. If you had a picture of the cat the hunter, you would still say it was a cat doing nothing, but there is a difference.

If you go into a store and approach the vacant thing at the checkout with an enquiry such as 'Excuse me, but do these adapters screw in or are they socketed?', then the look you receive can only confirm that you are addressing a farting cat. It must be impressed on everyone, especially your least able people, that they must tune in to the customers' conversation. Bright, enthusiastic and understanding. Just (and of course that is a big just) doing that will probably double your sales. I said less able, but the more able can be even more useless – even destructive of sales. How and why do you recruit people? I bet its always with a skill in mind. 'Wanted electrical engineer', 'computer programmer', 'head chef', 'HR manager.' What did you last fire someone for? Lack of skill? No. I bet it was for attitude, personality, or character. So why didn't you recruit them for that? The cliché for this is 'recruit for attitude and train for skill'. Which brings us nicely to the talking bottom. The oily salesperson sells us some piece of technical kit, with his silken tongue and weasel words. The following day it expires. Does the salesperson come to fix it? No, the talking bottom arrives. A thing with a box of tools in one hand and a dog mess firmly fixed to one shoe. The cheery greeting is 'Who sold you this then?'

'Derek.'

'Derek's a prat.' At which, this thing vanishes into our new treasure with only its bottom protruding, whereupon a muffled voice – which seems to emanate from said bottom – says things like 'They're all made in the Far East these. Not flippin' safe. Last one of these burnt the client's office down!'

Many of you at this point are saying 'Ho ho, that's just like my service department. They are little tinkers.'

They are more than little tinkers, they are destroying your business. You cannot afford to employ disloyal or surly staff. You must have people who enthusiastically promote your products and services. In previous books I have almost proudly stated how poor the British are at self promotion and loyalty. As I have said before, if we worked in a meat pie factory, there is one thing we would never eat. 'Don't eat one of those, I work there. We lost a rat the other day, I swear it went in the chicken and mushroom.' Then we are surprised when the company goes bust after the 'rat scare'.

ASK YOURSELF

Are your people **active**? *Are they alive and vigorous in their attitude to your customers? The posh name is* **active listening**.

Time has moved on and having everyone on side is now vital. They are either with us or against us, Ambassador or Assassin. Give engineers, service and parts people sales training, and more importantly make sure they apply it at every opportunity.

SYMBOL OF STATUS

So now our people have got information, what is the other benefit of asking questions? As we have been constantly referring to our front line people as ambassadors, it would be good if we could give them a bit more status. The higher the status, the more influence they will have over the customers' decisions. Perhaps you employ school kids as part-time staff. When do you use them? At your busy times, of course. When there are squillions of unrepeatable customer opportunities. Customers who believe they can ride roughshod over some 'daft kid'. If we could get that daft kid asking questions, we might just give them a bit of status because it is a fact that people who ask more questions tend to have more status. Remember those long hot boring summer days at school, the teacher would drone on about some boring thing or other as you become drowsy and inattentive? Perhaps you were gazing longingly at the world outside until … 'You! What was the name of Henry VIII's third wife?' When you snap back to the land of the living, just say to someone, 'May I ask you something?' and then remain silent, hunting cat style, waiting for a reply. That will not be long in coming and you will notice that you have their undivided attention. The look is that of a rabbit in the headlights. We tend to pay attention to people who ask questions, and people with status tend to ask more questions. Doctors, judges, police, and our own bosses. The opposite is also true in that people with low status tend to ask fewer questions. The repair person, receptionist or shop assistant all tend to start with 'Where's the machine?' or 'How may I help you?' Then it collapses into (to quote the war movies) 'we ask all the questions': 'How much are these?' and 'Do you have a room?' The more they are treated like minions, the more their status is reduced and the less likely it is they are able to influence the customers' decisions because, lets be clear, this is exactly what we want them to do. The customer care/focus bit, although important, was simply aimed at preventing our people from obstructing or pissing off our customers. Now we will get our people to actually create sales. We have started to let our customers buy, now we are going to GET them to buy and for that we need a bit of control.

TAKE CONTROL

So, on to the third benefit of questions and that is control. You want the customer to hear your sales story at your pace and in the right order. They bounce about saying 'Can you get these in yellow?' or 'I saw bigger ones down the road', and to less experienced people this can be most confusing and dispiriting, but all can be brought under control with 'Is it yellow you wanted?' or 'How would a bigger one help?'

As we saw in the furniture store story, that simple 'yep' or 'nope' was replaced by questions and the information we gained resulted in a sale, but there are more subtle forces at play here. The questions also seemed to create some kind of commitment or even obligation from the customer. This is because the more trouble you go to for the customer, the more likely they are to buy. An old radio store famously put their bestselling item on display in the front of their window. Although their stock room was brimming with these radios, if you came in to view one the staff were told to fetch it from the window. This would involve destroying the display and more than likely tearing the arse out of the assistant's trousers. They would arrive in front of you breathless, bleeding but victorious, grasping the radio like the spoils of war being presented to an emperor. Now tell me, are you going to say 'Nah, I don't want it. Now put it back'? You would be hard hearted if you did, and most people bought. Anyway, even if it lifted sales by ten per cent it was worth having. Of course the opposite is true; if people are not prepared to put themselves out at all, we feel absolutely no motivation to buy.

WHAT IF ...?

When you are interested in a car, they don't say 'There's no one here to help you at the moment,' but they do say 'We'll pop one round to you now for you to try.'

When you look at washing machines, they don't say, 'You can't have the one on display, and there aren't any in stock,' but they do say 'Of course you can have that one, but I can have a new boxed one delivered within the hour.'

When you have a repair done they don't say 'You really need this accessory, ring the office to see if they can sell you one,' but they do say 'I'll pop back to the warehouse and get one, and drop it off to you before lunch.' We find it very difficult to say 'no thank you' to these people.

OK now they have the information, the status, and the control, what do they do with it?

THE OLDEST TRICK IN THE BOOK

We have to dig into the past of selling to find the next steps. When the ancient tombs of Egypt were being excavated, in one of the oldest sarcophaguses a mummy was found. In its dust-dry hand a scroll was found. On it was written in hieroglyphics 'A.I.D.A.' The archaeologists had found the earliest example of a sales representative. Down the following centuries salespeople have been taught AIDA. Just because it is old and cheesy doesn't mean that it should be abandoned completely, because it contains a truth. The acronym stands for Attention, Interest, Desire, and Action.

Many books have been written about AIDA so we shall cut it as short as possible. Without people's full attention, the sale doesn't even start. That catchy advertisement may get your attention, the shouting market trader, the fish-throwing Americans, the window display or the employee that asks questions. Once the attention is secured, we must make the customer interested. They must see that the product or service is relevant and useful to them. This means talking about the benefits of our offering. Desire is about the mouth-watering improvements those benefits will bring to their lives. And last but most certainly not least, action. Proposing the action that will ensure the customer commits, signs or parts with money.

THOUGHT

Just because it is old, doesn't mean it doesn't work. Go to a second-hand bookshop and find ten, twenty, thirty, forty or fifty-year-old-or-more sales and business books. They will all contain forgotten gems.

This is not intended as a sales training book, but is intended to be a bit of a wild gallop through the new business culture, showing how you can survive and even prosper in it. BUT, (I know you knew there was going to be a but), if all your people don't sell, you have got an arm tied behind your back, and it really isn't rocket science. A simple understanding by everyone of Questions, the ancient AIDA, could net you millions.

THE OBJECT OF DESIRE

The Interest and Desire thing hovers around the contentious area of selling benefits. In sales guru circles, it is a real 'Angels on the Head of a Pin' issue. We might complicate things for your delectation later, but the simple 'Which means …' technique will work for the time being. Again, lets keep it simple. Remember my telly-selling hero: 'It's 100 Hz, which means the picture will be flicker free and that means for you cinema quality pictures.' The only problem is that this requires an acceptable level of product knowledge. That is also a great benefit later in the sale, but how many of your people understand your offer and can tie the customer to it? When did you last sit them all down with talk and chalk until they understood what it was they were offering? There is a famous story that I cannot recall precisely, but in essence it involves a CEO of a multi-national electronic company touring his production line. He spoke to a woman wiring operative and asked her what she thought of the product. She said that she had owned one of their company's steam irons for many years, and that it had been great. The boss nodded warmly, but later told one of his minions that he wasn't aware that they made irons. The minion replied that they didn't, they only made electronics for the telecoms industry. His employee who had worked for them for many years had quite cheerfully believed she was making domestic appliances. Not a great ambassador, but to be fair, a fairly unwitting assassin. It was our fault for not helping her to understand what she was involved in making and how, by enthusiastically promoting it, she could preserve or even enhance her job.

ASK YOURSELF

When did you last ask your people if they understood what business they were in? Do you give them history lessons (your history, of course)? Teach them 'why' not 'how'.

TIME FOR ACTION

The information is gathered, the benefits have the customer drooling with excitement. Now what? Time for ACTION. In the mummy's other hand was a book, resplendent in the title 'Closing the Sale'. So much old knackers has been spouted on the subject. An advert for salespeople even said 'wanted, good closers'. I suppose this came about because salespeople so often come away with nothing. The answer seemed to be that they failed to close the sale. Again, this is neither the time or place, but it is heresy to suggest that they may have been poor salespeople selling crap products at too high a price. In that case the sale hardly opens, let alone closes. For us, for now, the riches lie in getting our people to simply ask the customer to buy something.

The simplest way is to walk up to the customer and say 'buy something'. A little stark, a little unembellished, I know, but it is a start.

'Have a nice big slice of our freshly baked cake.'

'That would make a lovely present for someone.'

'Feed the birds, tuppence a bag.'

Its lack of subtlety means that some do not buy, but some do. The some that do are an addition to your current sales. So forget the unsophistication and bank the money. Remember our friend,

'Spare any change please'? He makes a good living just asking for money with no product or guarantee, and with no explanation.

Next level up from the bare-faced request is the subtle disguise of it. It is always nice to give the customer a choice. The problem has always been that very often the choice being yes or no, the answer tends to be 'no'. 'Do you need any help?' 'No'. 'Would you like one?' 'No.' 'Will there be anything else?' 'No.' We must prepare a choice so the customer can choose to do business with us, or could choose to do business with, er, well, us, actually.

'Did you want the red one or the blue?'

'Did you want it wrapped or will you take it like it is?'

'Shall we come and see you on Wednesday or would some time next week be better for you?'

A restaurant chain of my acquaintance just whacked out the good cheapo steak and chips. The waiting staff would ask 'Will there be anything else?' or 'Did you want to see the sweet menu?' Obviously there is a possible 'no' lurking here. We got them saying 'Would you like a sweet or coffee?' It immediately added a couple of million to the top line.

A TIP

Watch every customer contact and count how often your people ask for the business. Increase that number, increase your profit. Simple, huh?

PAUSE FOR THOUGHT

People obsess about the bottom line. If you look at a statement of account, it starts with the top line, SALES. This is written in a kind of surprised writ-in-stone sort of way. Then the whole of the rest of the statement is about how this fixed figure is eaten into. Wages, rents, vehicles, raw materials, interest payments: on and on it goes until you get to that good old bottom line, the one that counts, the one that changes. Only by mucking about with the figures between can that all-important bottom line be improved. Every business guru and consultant witters and drivels on about efficiency, flat organisations, cost control, but just think outside the box (to use jargon) for a moment. Why not increase the top line?

If the top line is huge enough, the Board Directors can light their cigars with hundred-dollar bills.

Possibly we should add just a whiff of sophistication to really make the sale complete. You will remember that we got our team asking questions partly to gather information. Well, now is the time to use it. What our people should do is to remind the customer of the key points and, as a consequence of those points, they should suggest action. The difficulty is that only the relevant and positive points are needed. The last thing we want to do is to remind the customer of the things that pissed them off. A storeman might say, 'You have told me that your current model leaks, you agree that the current bearings and seals are not up to the job, and that you are losing thousands in downtime every week. You have also agreed that the P4075 has to have heavy duty seals and bearings which would solve the leak problem, and that would mean no more downtime. (Wait for agreement.) Then may I suggest you take a P4075?' A bit glib, but I am sure you see how it works. Reading back over that last part, it all seems a bit too easy, and it does throw up a couple of concerns. First, can you get all of your people doing this, and if you can't, does it matter? Yes it does matter. It is absolutely vital. You cannot allow thick or disloyal people to rob you of an opportunity to make your enterprise profitable. Businesses only fail through a lack of sales. You may challenge this and hold up examples of companies who despite high sales still lost money, but it is hardly selling if you give the stuff away. Price is one of the things that has to be sold. People are either recruited just for their core skills, i.e., engineer, accountant, pilot or receptionist, or they are human table legs inasmuch as they passively hold up one corner. That part-time school kid at the superstore. Just a table leg. Sits at the till, takes the money. A dangerous experiment that is best only tried in theory is to take a market trader and put them into any part of your company – whether you are a lawyer, a steel merchant, or whatever. It won't be long before the customers pour in.

HE SCARED THE CRAP OUT OF ME

Years ago I did a project for a multi-millionaire who owned a chain of shops, but he had started out by market trading. We visited one of his stores on a wet Tuesday and, hardly surprisingly, there were no customers. 'What's going on?' he asked one of the staff. 'We're not very busy,' she whined. Like a whirlwind he started hauling stock off the shelves and handing it out. I got a woven rug. 'Follow me', he cried. We all set off into the street, whereupon he started accosting astonished shoppers. 'There you are madam, just feel that, come on now, doesn't that feel lovely? Wouldn't you be proud to own this?' He certainly got their attention. People were literally herded into the shop until it was packed out, and soon the tills were ringing.

FROM BOTTOM TO TOP

My second worry concerns the position of the people concerned. I have bandied about phrases such as table legs, and part-time kids, but what about senior partners, managers, and directors? They are even more difficult to motivate to sell, either believing it to be beneath them, or not relevant. The shame is that their level of authority makes them ideally positioned to lift that top line. The senior lawyer who says, 'You've agreed that the new employment laws are a minefield, your take-over bid for this company will mean a lot more people and a lot more problems. You have said that you wish you could forget the legal stuff, so I think it would be a good idea if I introduced you to our employment specialist, and he can ...'

Beneath them or not, don't lawyers need more business and the revenue it brings?

We have to go out and grab that business. Even in bad times, it can save us if we sell a hundred, and our competitors sell a hundred, and the recession causes a 25 per cent drop in business which makes both uncompetitive. Then go and take their customers, leaving them no sales, and you 150. Better off than when you started.

THOUGHT

One of the clichéd ways to stay competitive is price. The accepted wisdom is that if you are not a famous brand, you may have to sharpen your pencil when it comes to price, but just to wind things up a little may I suggest that under certain circumstances customers will choose to pay a higher price. Take a holiday brochure. Select a simple destination, look at the descriptions of the accommodation – all glowing praise, every one. One is priced at £750 for the week, the other £925. When you visit the travel agent to book, I bet the £925 one is sold out. The reason may be obvious. It is because the higher price raises expectations, but it is interesting to note that once away from brand pressure, the customer freely chooses the dearer option. What then reduces that willingness is experience. As soon as the customer comes into contact with us, we get the opportunity to disappoint and frustrate. Slow, uninformed staff, late delivery, lack of interest, failure to deliver. Perhaps we should stop having any contact with out customer until we are ready, with people who can raise value rather than reduce it. Branding has become the lazy way out, people will fight their way past lazy, unhelpful staff to get their hands on a brand, but brands are only a pivot point, a benchmark. Again with no people involved, price can work the magic. If we had a shelf of trainers with NIKES at £100 and our own brand Speedysure, they would have to be sold at £25 despite the fact that they were made of the same material and come from the same part of the world as the NIKES. But a little further along, set aside from the others, a pair of trainers signed 'Designed by Peter Van Tolenberg' complete with limited numbers on a bronze tag and a book of instructions on care and maintenance are an eye watering £400. I bet you will sell some. I just made the name up. The brand was the benchmark and you can shoot above or below. Dumb selling at its best. You may find this section's obsession with expecting the least from people a little offensive, but the aim is to get the minimum standard for everyone. The reasons may be to compensate for a lack of talent, ability, intelligence, attitude or it may be that technical or administrative people are too busy to manage anything more. Whatever the answer, they certainly shouldn't do any less. The least able team member could easily manage this, in fact let's look at your most stupid and mindless team member. The computer, or more precisely, the Web site.

The common perception is 'bought on the Web equals cheap'. But what if the Web site could sell? Currently most Web sites are just catalogues on TV instead of paper. Catalogue shopping over the wires. It is not surprising it has ground to a bit of a halt, after all you can only do so much mail order, but the power of IT can way exceed that miserable task. There has been a quest for many years for artificial intelligence. To be fair, a hopeless task considering that normal intelligence is as rare as hens' teeth in most enterprises. A sort of breakthrough came long before computers became powerful because a psychologist realised that if you simulated questions, listening and sympathy, the simplest machine could give the impression of intelligence. It pretended to be a medical diagnostic machine. 'How are you today, are you well?' Y/N. 'No.' 'Oh dear, what seems to be the matter?' You replied. Then: 'I'm sorry to hear that. Has it been like that for long?' People thought the thing a genius, a kind, trustworthy genius in fact. With the new power at our fingertips, we could go further. Imagine I am going through the Web to find a cheap holiday when I come to a site called 'just-the-jolly-holiday-for-you.org'. The screen says 'Hello Geoff, what can I do for you?' 'I would like a holiday.' 'Smashing, what do you enjoy doing?' 'I would like to try a bit of sailing, but mostly relaxing.' 'Sounds fun, what about weather?' 'Oh, sunny.' 'Mmm, let me think, sunny, relaxing and perhaps a bit of sailing – how about food?' 'I love Italian food.' 'OK, how about the Hotel Splendid, Lake Maggiorri? Would you like to see tonight's menu? Would you like a video link to Carlo Capriccio, the Head Waiter? This is Doris and Fred Smith, they have just stayed there. Would you like to email them to see what they thought of it?' 'Yes, yes, yes.'

It is just the holiday for me, and I will pay full whack for it. The selling Web site got a good price. Not only does it prove a simple machine can sell, it also shows that everyone else shouldn't find it difficult.

CONCLUSION
If your sale is so simple that a dumb machine can do it, then:
- *people have no excuse not to do it every time; and*
- *your dumb machine should be doing it.*

SELL MORE

We can make the odds better by finding easy people to sell to. The easiest people of all are the customers we already have. Almost all of us fail to sell enough to our customers. To say that selling more than the customer or client expected can frighten them off is indefensible. The truth is the more we sell, the more likely we are to keep them. Marketing people witter on ad nauseam about market share, at best a total irrelevance, at worst a sodding great millstone. Take the privatised utilities and the big telecoms companies, they have huge market share, but it is all rump end stuff. It is like having a cherry, and when everyone has stolen all the ripe juicy flesh, saying 'We have retained ownership of the stone and stalk which is our core business and represents 80 per cent of the original cherry's worth.' (Now that's something I had never noticed before, 'CORE'. We always talk about core business but in all other parts of life, the core is what is left after the good bits have gone. I chuck the cores away.) Let's examine instead customer share. What percentage of this person's entire spend do we get our hands on? He bought his bolts from us, but his nuts, washers, and spanners elsewhere. We might have 65 per cent of the bolt market, but the profit is in the spanners. Also, if customers spread their business they have a great opportunity to sample the competition. I have bought insurance from the same broker for years, mostly because of inertia, but we got to first name terms. When my son went away to college I asked them if they did student insurance. 'Nah, isn't worth it. There is a firm that specialises in it and we can't touch them. Go and see them.' Well, I suppose they were helpful pointing me in the right direction. I visited this new company – somewhere I would never have thought of going. By jingo, they had delicious free coffee, fresh cheery offices, and happy staff. 'How much?' 'Twenty quid, sir.' 'Gosh, that's reasonable.' 'How much are you currently paying for your household policy, sir?' GAME OVER.

In another incident, I was visiting a large American department store shortly after one of my books had come out, and vanity dictates you always have to try and buy a copy. I asked in the book department. 'Let me look for you, sir. We don't have one left on display right now, but if you have a complimentary coffee in our lounge, I will get one from stock and have it wrapped for you.' As I sat sipping my coffee, I saw someone legging it up the road with a bundle of bills. Obviously off to the local bookshop to get a copy of the book. A no profit exercise maybe but the customer didn't escape to sample the opposition. Again, this gives small companies a chance to win. Could you imagine Woolworth's saying 'Drop back in five minutes and we will have one for you', and then whipping up the road to buy one? But *you* could do it.

A TIP

Go for 100 per cent of every customer's potential spend.

I LOVE CUSTOMERS WHO SPEND

At one time there was a lot of talk about add-on or link selling. Years ago if you worked in a shoe shop you would have probably been trained by someone with a North London accent who would say, 'Now boys and girls, don't forget your add-ons,' which meant, in essence, that whenever you bought a pair of shoes, a great dollop of a thing would leap out and shriek 'Do you want any polish?' to which you would cry 'No.' To be fair even that crude and intrusive approach increased sales by about 15 per cent. Companies would construct products to be add-ons. Fancy care sprays, special packaging, and let us not forget today's plague, the hugely expensive extra guarantee. As I have already mentioned, the old fashion retailer indulged in the arcane art of accessorising which meant if you bought the shoes, then the handbag, hat, gloves, belt and brooch would be introduced. It has all died out through a lack of skill from the staff, just at the time when it is needed the most, because in this complicated old world the customer can no longer understand (nor, to be fair, do they want to understand) what it is they want or need. As we have seen before, the complications of life mean that if we want to enjoy all aspects of it, we must trust people to advise us on what would suit us best and bring us the most enjoyment. When we have found well-informed, trustworthy people, and they help us to purchase more than we anticipated, are they flogging the extras? I don't believe they are. They can be anyone from the part-time student I saw in a US car rental place, who helped every customer with the correct insurance and encouraged them to take a more comfortable car, raising every order value by about 80 per cent (but unless you understand the American public liability laws, he is doing you a big favour), through to a top corporate lawyer who after conducting you through a multi-million-pound leverage buyout, then introduces you to the partner who will ensure your future success and legal stability.

What are they doing, if not selling? They are actually doing something that is extremely customer friendly. Through great product knowledge and, more importantly, knowing how to apply and benefit from those products, they are ANTICIPATING THE CUSTOMER'S NEEDS. You see a customer with a garden hose, have they got the fittings? You see an order for valves to be sent to the desert; how about gaskets and extra pipework? You audit a new company's books. Have they made provision for the future? In every one of these cases, your expertise will result in the customer spending more and thanking you with tears in their eyes that they did. It should be your honourable duty to anticipate your customers' needs.

KNOWLEDGE IS POWER

The key, when it comes to ALL your people, is product knowledge. Are they knowledgeable?

My central heating pump had failed at 4.30 on a Friday. I rang the manufacturer and got 'Gatehouse!'

'Can I speak to technical, please?'

'This is the Gatehouse. They've all gone home.'

'Great!'

'Can I help you with anything?'

'I doubt it, but …' I unburdened myself.

'Well I can despatch you a new one, but may I suggest you upgrade to an 85? That'll prevent cavitation, you know.'

The next day a parcel arrived with my new pump, which a few minutes later was humming away quietly and efficiently. I spent twice as much as I had intended to, and was doing a loopy dance of happiness around my now warm boiler.

KNOW THE DRILL AND EXTRACT THE MONEY

I was once asked if any business could benefit from being sales aware. I think one of the strangest I ever worked with was dentists, but on reflection, they are a perfect case. We entirely trust them, we understand nothing of their business and yet they break every rule in the book. Talk about lack of eye contact. They wear a stuffing great mask, for Pete's sake. You lie there with your gob jammed open while they poke and prod about inside, all the while uttering mysterious numbers to their assistant. 'Gingival 17, occluded 4, bipolaratic cavities 7,' they mumble, then add 'won't be a minute,' and after some mixing and stirring, they start treatment.

They came to me because they said that no one bought the expensive treatments. The solution was easy. We taught the dentists how to sell. After the poking and prodding, the dentists were taught to sit and face the patient, remove the mask and say 'Well, it all seems mostly OK, there is a little damage that I would normally fill, but a lot of people don't like those big black fillings. Did you know it is possible to restore the whole tooth with a white enamel filling?' Await the reply, then: 'By the way, have we explained the techniques of veneers to you?'

I won't bother you with the whole gory business, but suffice to say sales rose by a very large percentage – not because of anything clever, but because patients simply had never been asked or given the options before. Next time you speak to a customer or client or answer an enquiry, don't just say yes or no, review their options, anticipate their needs, and then ASK THEM TO BUY.

NEXT

THE TIMES THEY ARE A CHANGIN'

To move forward now we need to change. Ain't that a classic line from just about every business book you have ever read? Why do we need to change? Again we have to be careful we don't get sucked in by the business gurus' good old one-liners. The problem is the bigger the bestselling guru book is, the cleverer but more meaningless the bollocksey old one-liners are, and on the subject of change there are some absolute corkers. My favourite is 'you don't have to change, after all survival isn't compulsory'. Ho ho, what a wag, straight to the heart of the matter. That pulls us up and makes us think, but hang on a moment, do things like that change our lives? Should we share these nuggets with our chums? Should we leap from the cupboard at parties crying 'If you want to soar with the eagles, don't hang round with the turkeys', or 'Don't lets discuss the past, lets discuss the future because that is where we are going to spend the rest of our lives'? If you did, I bet you wouldn't get invited to many parties. To be fair, it is meaningless drivel, but with a bit of modification that phrase on change can become meaningful.

'You don't have to change.' That's right, you don't. Another piece of infuriating old tosh is this work/life balance crap, meaning that if you have such a harsh, intolerable, unremittingly dull job that it either kills you, sends you bonkers or makes you leave, your employers won't get the best from you and will fail to drain every vital drop of your precious juices. The work/life balance is created to give you just enough relaxation and life outside work to stop you running amok but, at the same time, the ruthless, beating, whip-cracking slave-drivers who keep us chained to our oars are saying that we must be prepared to change. It is a bit like nailing an LCD screen to the back of the rower in front of you so you can have in-galley entertainment. The truth is that the biggest change an employee can make is to stride into their employer's office and say 'You can shove your job up your arse,' but that isn't necessarily the change they had in mind. What they were thinking of was less money, more complicated technology, or strange work patterns. So even if you own the company, why change? All businesses have a finite life. If you made horse bridles, gas mantles or lamp wicks, your sun would have set. The gurus would have said that you had failed to change, but as you sit in the Bahamas with the 40 million quid you had made, you probably wouldn't give a toss.

ASK YOURSELF

Forget change for a moment, are you enjoying your life? Do you have loads of laughs? Would you die for your career? Are you tempted to say 'stuff it' and lie on a beach somewhere? In other words, be sure the changes are not guru-driven, boss-driven or job-driven, but are about you being happy. If you are not happy, then consider change.

THE PAIN OF CHANGE

Why change? Employer or employee, there is a finite shelf life to, well, life itself. Make a few quid, a penny more than you can spend, then relax. The only time to change is if the world around you changes enough to threaten this idyllic future. Change is horrible, it hurts, it disrupts, it upsets, only do it if the pain of not changing is greater than the pain of changing.

NO ONE LISTENS, NO ONE CHANGES

That is why writing books like this is a bit odd because every guru's hope and, I suppose, fear is that the reader takes the advice on board and changes. If you think that change is not a problem for you, an amusing exercise that was suggested by another guru may bring the situation into focus. Just try sitting in a different chair to watch TV. See the chaos that causes. Try sleeping on the other side of the bed if you want to get your throat cut. The problem is that we form habits in seconds. When I do the different chair line at conferences, I get a polite chuckle and everyone goes out to get a coffee, but when they come back there is always a huge shemozzle with 'Excuse me, I think I was sitting there', and 'That's my chair'. They have been in some scabby hotel for an hour and already they have taken ownership of 'their chair' and formed a habit. We are all creatures of habit. Starting a business or a new job is a bit like coming down the slip road on to a busy motorway. It is terrifying, we have to quickly get up to speed and barge our way into the mêlée while we exchange abuse with our fellow motorists, but it isn't long before we get up to speed. Into the fast lane we go at 70 or 80 miles an hour and we start to relax. Maybe make a phone call or two, open our sandwiches, or think about our holiday plans. In short, we are cruising. The problem is we hear no alarm bells, feel no shock or pain as we go sailing past our turning. It is not until we reach a sign that says 'Glasgow, four miles' that we think 'That's a long way from Birmingham'. There are so many enterprises that have missed their turn off. It is not so much change as taking back control of what is happening to us. Make things happen instead of letting things happen. Hunter, not prey. The gurus say 'We should learn to listen', the company says 'We listen to our people and our customers.' I write 'Dear Sir, your products are crap and your staff are surly gits.' They reply 'Thank you for your kind letter, but you are mistaken. Our focus group and the result of exhaustive surveys assure us we are doing a great job.' Kind, caring, people-focused companies listen, dictators don't. Wrong! Unsuccessful people don't listen, successful people do – wicked dictator or not. Stalin listened. He had a huge mechanism for listening to his people called the KGB. Oh boy, they listened alright. People believe despots fail because they are despots, but they don't, they fail because they become complacent. They have forgotten where they were going and have listened to the hangers-on and sycophants. Whether you are a benign democracy or dictatorship you have to search for the truth or it will sneak up and bite you. If our world is coming to a premature end before we have stashed enough money away to get out of the rat race, we must find out what is going wrong and, unpalatable though it might be, we must then consider change.

A DARE

Listen to what people really say about you and decide whether to change or bugger off.

I'LL CHANGE WHEN I KNOW I AM PERFECT

Now we have a little paradox because on one hand we can see change is often a painful process that is best avoided, and we can agree that we should only change if things are looking bad. BUT then it could be too late. There we have it, change is horrible, we shouldn't change unless we have to, but the very best time to change is before we have to. However, if everything is going well, why change? Why not change at a time of despair, destruction and despondency? Because we won't feel like it then, that's why. Our capacity for energy and enthusiasm is like a flask of fizzing Perrier water. After a good night's kip you wake invigorated, full of vim and vigour ready to face the day. That fizzy flask is 100 per cent full, bubbling over with enthusiasm. Then the phone rings. 'That stuff you sent by air is leaking some kind of funny sticky stuff.' 'You know that big account that owes us all that money? They've gone bust.' 'Brian's not coming in, he's got diarrhoea through a hole in his shoe.' So by about … … five past nine you are feeling drained and that flask is down to 50 per cent and you tend to bump along through the rest of the day on half power. Unless of course it is one of those days that gets even worse and you hear that your mother-in-law has been in a huge crash and has walked out without a scratch! That finishes you off. Drained to nothing. The flask is at 0 per cent. It just isn't worth going on any more. Now let me ask you, when would be the best time to do stuff, to try those new ideas? I bet you can see that when the fizzing bottle is full and frothing, running at 100 per cent, that must be the very best time to throw yourself into a new project, to take a different direction. If you can see the logic of that, then you would be the sort of person who can stand naked in front of the bedroom mirror, admiring the taut thighs, the firm flat stomach, the tight well-formed chest, not an inch of flab to mask those healthy rippling muscles. Gazing at this picture of perfection, you muse to yourself 'Mmmm, I think I'll go on a diet'. Do you really do that or are you like me? When I run naked across my bedroom and discover I have carpet burns on my arse, that is when I go on a diet – driven by despair and humiliation to consider change. The problem is that if we change at that 0 per cent point, it is often too late and we are so low that we don't have the energy to cope. OK, you don't have to change, but if you decide to it is best to be fully equipped to handle it.

THE POINT

Change is easier when you are feeling good, so it may be better to jump before you are pushed.

A VERY STUPID FROG

Of course change can be thrust upon us by events, perhaps the markets move, our product is no longer competitive. The trouble is that more often than not, we don't see it coming. Charles Handy, and then a number of others, have been taken with the idea of the boiled frog. I thought the idea of boiling frogs was very jolly and, in an earlier book, I also leapt upon the boiling frog band-wagon. Some time later, someone pointed out that my interpreta-tion, apart from being more gory, had drawn a different conclu-sion from everyone else. My main point I suppose is that the frog is stupid and everyone else says it is the hapless victim of circum-stance. There is another book on change that totally bewilders me, called 'Who Moved my Cheese?' So, to clear the air, let's boil the frog again and serve it up with a bit of moving cheese. For this experiment, you will need a large strong metal bucket. Go off into a swamp somewhere, and find a large healthy frog, sitting in its pond, going 'Ribbit! Ribbit!' What you have to do is to gently scoop this frog into the bucket, taking with it plenty of pond water. As long as the frog has not been spooked, it should be content sit-ting surrounded by its familiar environment, ergo the pond water. We must then take this bucket, and resident thereof, back home. Place the bucket on the stove and turn the heat up to maximum. After a little while, small bubbles will form at the bottom of the bucket, but the frog will still cheerfully sit there going 'Ribbit!' The water starts to steam and the bubbles grow, but still the frog sits going 'Ribbit!' Eventually you get a good rolling boil and the frog bobs to the surface, white flesh, eyes blank, steam from every ori-fice, dead, cooked. The question then posed is how did the frog allow itself to be cooked? On revisiting this story I now know where the different interpretation may occur. I believe that the original point is that as the frog's environment gradually changes, it fails to notice these gentle incremental changes – end of point. But I then feel compelled to ask what should the frog have done?

When I ask this question at conferences, the answer is always 'It should have jumped out.' 'When?' 'When the water got hot.' 'How hot?' In your current position – a little bit of warmth or a few bubbles like some keenly priced foreign imports, finding different suppliers, the law changing, new technology – do you jump? Not until it is too late, you don't. Actually, while writing this it dawned on me that this is a fairly stupid story. Another illustration of how the guru can mislead us with clever stories (me included) because if you think about it, the frog would be stupid to leap out of a safe environment at the first steamy bubble type sign of trouble. He only looks stupid to us because we, in our god-like overview of the bucket, know what outcome is expected. I used to suggest that one should take a frog every week and boil it until you get bored with it. (If this frog boiling thing is upsetting you, any domestic pet will do, but I'm not sure about hamsters – they seem to know and I think they would get out if they could. It's the pathetic scrab-bling at the side of the bucket that always gives the game away!) The frogs never ever try to get out, so to add a bit of spice to the proceedings I suggested flipping a coin – heads you live, tails you die. 'Flick', tails – the gas stays on. 'Flick', heads – the gas goes off. At this point, interview the frog. It should greet you with tears of gratitude. 'Thank you,' it should weep, 'You saved my life!' It doesn't say that, it says 'There you are, the gas has gone off. I told you, if you sit tight the heat would die down. I've been in hot water before. It didn't do me any harm. It made me strong!' You want to tell it what a stupid frog it is and that it had nothing to do with its own survival, but the problem is that the only frogs we can talk to are the live ones. The boiled ones' lips are sealed. Liv-ing, experienced frogs will therefore tell you to sit tight. The story, I suppose, is to invite us to change when we see the signs. Yes, I'll have a bit of that, but the signs of what? In the bucket game, we play the part of ruthless incomprehensible fate and, as you read, mighty forces are lifting your bucket onto the stove. Sure, if our comfortable environment starts to become uncomfortable, and the signs are there, the writing is on the wall. We should change sooner rather than later, but one issue that never comes up in all this change stuff is the concept of fun, vigour, excitement, taking control, having a laugh, taking some risks, pissing on someone's yucca plant, shoving a sodding great huge fizzing firework through life's letterbox and running off laughing like a maniac. Consider just two states of being, either living in the sun – eating, sleeping, and bobbing about in the warm ocean like a happy turd, or doing things to make it happen, trying new stuff. The in-between stable existence is a living death. They say a rut is just a grave that is open at both ends. Forget boiling frogs, consider change because you fancy doing something different. In the clever little book on change, 'Who Moved my Cheese?' life for the hero consists of two little folk, and two mice who leave their homes each day to retrieve cheese from the same place in a maze each day. Disaster strikes when the cheese runs out and the mice and one of the folk were brave enough to depart from the routine and search for new cheese, despite their fears. People tell me how much they gained from the book, but as soon as I started it I thought 'Where will I find the pickled onions? I'm bored with cheese.' I wouldn't be arsed to go into the maze long before the cheese ran out, but would be searching for some chicken madras, something with a kick, something to get out of bed for. Either rest in contentment, or go out and make things happen.

THOUGHT

If you can't change fate, why not consider change for the pure excitement of it? If nothing else, it will truly piss off and scare your chums.

DOGGY STYLE

I suppose that's how I came to business guru-ing, through sales. Real, old fashioned, creative (as in creating sales, not painting or sculpting) salespeople actually made things happen. They took empty order books and filled them. They took the unsellable and sold them. They could build that top line so high, that even the most stupid directors in the world couldn't lose money.

Recently I had cause to spend a day or two with a company that was owned and run by a tough gritty guy who had come from the toughest of direct sales environments. He had done it all, washing machines, double glazing, the lot. He was now involved in one of the new-era, high-technology companies in a sector that, at the time of writing, is going through a totally torrid time. Some of the biggest names are in the 90 per cent club – in other words, 90 per cent has been wiped off their share values. A lot of them are also my valued clients, but when I visit them it is like a fabulous university campus with cosy meeting rooms, loads of knee grasping, herbal tea and thoughts about the universe. There are HR meetings, strategy meetings, anger counsellors, team building, exercises, the gurus are stacked ten deep, and the band plays while they sink below the waves. This guy, however, hasn't even noticed a downturn. They prosper despite the crisis, raising profits year on year. How? They sell! They sell and they sell and they sell. The technological products are brought in and they sell them. They start with a hundred eager kids who just pound away at the phones, making appointments. How many times have you told people like that to sod off? Despite the rejection, they plug away. They average 20 appointments a day and those are then pushed on to the tough, hard-bitten sales force, who constantly moan that the appointments aren't strong enough, but still they sell to 20 per cent. I know it's a crude, brutal numbers game, but they are winning it while the famous names have boiled in their buckets. I will admit that their environment made me feel uneasy and I would probably tone down their aggression. But be sure, if you could hire them to attack your market, whether you are a lawyer, bearing maker or confectioner, it would not be long before you had more work than you could handle at any price that you would care to name. Maybe we can't buy the whole tough package, but we should consider taking a leaf from their book. We want to make things happen. I love the idea of making success inevitable. I look at my product or service and decide who should be using them. If they are not today, then they will be tomorrow. In a previous book I used the model of a sheepdog as the perfect sale, and it still delights me. If you watch a dog herding sheep, you just need to ask yourself what the sheep would do if the dog rushed at them barking. The answer is, of course, that they would scatter. Just like the pushy salesperson who rushes at us barking and howling, their opening benefits statements and all the other rubbish just makes us want to run and hide. Because of that we believe that we should indulge in the opposite kind of behaviour, but what would the sheep do if the dog wandered up to them and said, 'Oh, hi sheep. It's really nice of you to see me, there is a pen at the bottom of the field if you would like to shut yourselves in it, but anyway I'll leave a brochure of the wide range of pens available and my card. Please feel free to carry on grazing, but bleat if you need anything'?

The dog scampers off and writes 'Saw sheep – V. Interested, but need to speak to their ram before decision.'

The sheep are left bewildered, unmoved and thinking 'Who on earth was that?' What really happens is that the shepherd commands the dog with all sorts of whoops and whistles and shouts. The dog surveys the scene, the job in hand. There are the sheep, and away in the distance is the pen that they have to be taken to. The sheep are here and the pen is there and between these points are a number of obstacles – maybe a prickly hedge, a stream, a thicket of trees, gateposts and some marshy ground. At this point the dog doesn't do what we are tempted to do and come back to the shepherd whinging 'Oh wow, it's a really bad scene, the sheep are ill tempered and aggressive, there are loads of obstacles between them and the pen, and they are refusing to be interested.' What the dog does is to set off and herd the sheep. Perhaps because a dog is simple-minded, it isn't daunted or depressed, it just gets on with it.

POINT

If you can see a clear route and the obstacles are obvious, as long as you don't kid yourself, success will be inevitable.

FONDLE MY BOTTOM

Before going on much further, I am sure you see the analogy between customers and sheep, but the real point is to think very simply and pragmatically about people who aren't currently doing business with us. Just like the sheep, that is where they are now. Just there, not doing business with us. They may hate us, they may have never heard of us, they may not like what they have heard of us, the may not give a toss one way or the other, but that is where they are, and that is their position. That position is not doing business with us. The pen, if you like, is the position where they ARE doing business with us. There is a gap between these two positions and we need to take that potential customer from one position to the other. In that gap there are obstacles, but instead of bushes and streams, we get 'we did business with you before and you were crap', 'very nice but they are too expensive', 'we are very happy with the people we are using'. Classically these, in selling terms, are referred to as 'objections'. Many books have been written on handling objections. If you want to know more, try reading my book 'Resistance is Useless' where I deal with the subject at length, but as this book is about thinking differently, lets think differently about objections. As you may remember, the modern enterprise is supposed to be developing a relationship with its clients. With that in mind, I have to consider what an objection is. If you wanted to fondle my bottom, I may (only may) object, but that IS an objection. People may object to uninvited fondling, but if I can't afford something, can't understand something or worry that something will break, I am not objecting, I am expressing a concern. If I find someone to trust who can be my trusted advisor, they would listen to my concerns, sympathise with them and then put my mind at rest by explaining the solution to my worries. By the way, here we go again, that word TRUST. Empowerment needs trust, our people have to trust us, we must trust our people, and if we could win our clients' and customers' trust, life would get an awful lot easier. I suppose, strangely, the sheep must trust the dog or they would bugger off. The problem with classic objection handling is that it deflects, diminishes or dismisses the objection. If those objections are, as I believe, genuine concerns, the customers just shut up and determine to seek revenge later. This is usually by not buying, but if on the other hand by listening to those concerns and worries and then by using our knowledge and experience we can satisfy those concerns, it actually strengthens the relationship. Actually, while we are at it, we may consider this idea of the potential customer's starting position which, at the moment, is the position of *not* doing business with us. There are some very important points to make here. Firstly, until we know exactly where the sheep are or, in other words, what position they are in, we don't know where to start from, what obstacles stand in our way or how far to herd them. The clever company will ask a series of position questions, 'Who does this at the moment? Who did you use before? Why does this cause you problems? How could we help to solve them?' Another point worth making is that we shouldn't be depressed if the customer is miles away from us, or even if they hate us. It can give us a reason to talk.

I watched an American guy who called himself 'Mr Appointment' or something like that. He claimed that he could show anyone how to make appointments. His party trick at conferences was to throw telephone directories into the audience and then ask if anyone wanted an appointment.

'Sir, what is your company?'

'Lightening, Risk, and Promise.'

'Would you like an appointment tonight?'

'Yes please!'

'OK. You guy with the directory, pick a name at random.'

'Mackenzie.'

'OK, put his number through the P.A.' The whole audience of about five thousand sales people heard those dialling tones. Click, click.

'Mackenzie, waddya want?'

'Ah, Mr Mackenzie, I am ringing you from Lightening, Risk, and Promise.'

'Lightening, Risk, and Promise! You bastards killed my brother!'

The audience held their breath in gleeful anticipation, but our hero didn't even break step. 'I heard about that, Mr Mackenzie, and I felt it was time someone came to see you about it. How about Tuesday, or would next week be better?'

The very fact that the potential client hates you can give a good reason to see them. What happens then can admittedly become just a little exciting.

THINK ABOUT

Have the courage to find out how far you are from doing business with people. What is pissing them off? Then the decision whether or not you do anything about it is in your hands.

I was watching a CRM consultant the other day. Boy, did he talk bollocks. But one thing he said that was half true was that if it cost one pound to keep a customer then it costs ten pounds to find a new one. Yep, I agree with that, but then he said 'but it could cost a hundred pounds to recover a lost one'. I don't think so, lost customers can be a rich seam. They might find their new supplier is worse than you were but are too embarrassed to come back. A bit of cost effective grovelling on your part can often win them back, and the returned strays often stay loyal after the rigors of wandering. Go back through the files and be courageous; even if you killed their brother they might have cooled down a bit, and there is nothing to lose by chatting to them. Thirty percent recovered is not unusual and if you think that the average company loses 25 per cent of its customers each year, by going back three years into your records, you could increase business by 100 per cent.

FIND THE LOST

Of course, that is wildly optimistic because unless there has been a flaming great row, we don't know who the missing customers are or where they went. Of course that would be real CRM, where we could even track all our lost sheep. Imagine you have stopped using 'Wherever Holidays' because they had become a bit crap. Two years down the line they call you (not one of these ignorant calls that are unaware of your dissatisfaction – those are infuriating). 'We heard why you don't come on holiday with us. We are so sorry you became disappointed, but we know why and have made changes in response to your worries. Please give us another try – we promise you will be delighted.'

Sure, they had better have improved, but it is hard to resist that approach.

STAY IN CONTROL

OK, our dog has realised that the obstacles are concerns not objections, and while retaining control, has steered the sheep around them. Some people feel that I might be straying towards the boarders of pushy, but most sales fail when we lose control. If I simply have the intelligence of a dog, I can be in control without being pushy. The dog knows its sheep. It knows the lazy ones need a nip. 'Look, you have agreed all the points, I think the best thing is to have it installed so you can start making some money forthwith.' The dog also knows if you nip the nervous ones, you terrify them so it backs off until they are calm, but it stays in control. 'I think that covers all the ground for today, so I will leave this with you for you to try. Then we can get together later on. Do you have your diary?'

'DO YOU HAVE YOUR DIARY?' How many calls did you leave with the next appointment in the bag? CAREFUL CONTROL MAKES SUCCESS INEVITABLE.

FELL AT THE LAST

Imagine that dog doing all the work, miles of ground from one position to the next, dealing with each obstacle as it comes up until it arrives at the gate of the pen. It scampers back to the shepherd excited and thrilled. 'Well, boy, are they in the pen?' 'No, but they are very interested!' Fallen at the last hurdle. As we have discussed, this would have been described as a failure to close the sale or, as I call it, failure to progress action, but a great number of you are trying to win major contracts. There is a lot of old knackers spouted about getting to see the decision maker. A nice get-out because, if you cock things up, you could say that your victim wasn't the decision maker. The problem with big deals is that there probably isn't one decision maker anyway. I can think of at least three and you need to win them all, but if what you sell is worth thousands or even millions, it is worth making the effort. Imagine you make the world's fastest biscuit-making machine, with auto-cherry application functions. Your first decision maker may be the production or managing director (because you went to the top). You may think that double speed and half staff will appeal, and the job is done and dusted. You will get a bit miffed when that order doesn't come, but you neglected the other decision makers. What about the person who uses it? Head cherry-sticker. You have just done them out of a job.

Of course they won't say that to the boss, they will talk about difficulty of use and the threat of constant breakdown. We have to see them and include them. Make them see that they can improve their status and gain the boss's approval. From cherry-sticker to head of mechanical biscuit throughput. The person who quadrupled biscuit output. Then those who are paying for the thing. The finance department will go ape when they see the price of the thing, they have to believe the future return will make their figures and consequently them, look good. Notice none of them, however convinced, can sign the order on the spot. So what is the close to go for? What action? The answer is to propose the maximum action that person is qualified to take. 'OK, you agree it is easy to use, it can double your production, and will prevent those gits in despatch blaming you for quality. Then will you attend a meeting with your CEO, and the Finance Director to discuss details?' That is the best they can do. Just as a matter of interest, I often visit a fourth person – someone I can cultivate as a mole, anyone from van driver, supervisor, personal assistant. I need to hear things like: 'Mr Perkins, our buyer, hates people who wear blue', 'Go carefully with the thick kid in production, he is the boss's son', 'We had a PT45R and it burned the warehouse down'. It is called gathering intelligence and if you have a mole inside it prevents ambushes and elephant traps.

THE POINT
There may be a lot of people involved in your success (or your downfall, for that matter). Make sure you cover all of them.

POSTMAN'S KNOCK

It all builds into a cool and calculating plan for success. Target the clients you want and know you will get them. Win back the lost customers, and hang on to the current customers forever. Who is involved in this process? *Everybody.* When you have distilled this essence, you must sell this idea to all of your people. Everyone must be involved, everyone must sell, everyone must make it easier for your people to do business with, but you must listen to everyone.

I did a job for the Post Office a few years ago, and was speaking to the front line postmen and women. I commented on how complicated the parcel weighing was and how the price rose in penny increments. A parcel could cost £3.87, which may mean three £1 stamps, one 50p stamp, three 10p stamps, one 5p stamp and two 1p stamps. I asked why they didn't use 50p price bands, and a postwoman said 'Why have stamps at all? When you pay the machine prints out a receipt. If a part of that was sticky, it could be stuck on a parcel.' Another chipped in and said you could put a credit card in a slot and that could print out the postage, and another said the weighing point could be like a cash dispenser outside, and you could post parcels twenty four hours a day. At the time of writing this, Post Office counters don't even accept credit cards. Perhaps they should listen to their staff.

If this book is about anything, it is about how people can make a difference. HR's big bit of bullshit is the Dilbert-ridiculed statement 'people are our most valuable asset'. Make no mistake, they can be your biggest liability as well. Each person involved in

POINT

Talk to your people,
they have great ideas.

your enterprise (including you) is a miniature model of the business itself, like a fractal. Handled properly they can add value to everything. Do it wrong and they destroy value. AMBASSADOR OR ASSASSIN.

ABANDON ALL HOPE

Companies find adding value so hard that they abandon it, and to my horror some branches of this new religion called CRM actually encourage it. Returning to this half-wit who was being paraded as the prophet of CRM, they suggested that quality and service could be dumped if one could determine through CRM that the customers were driven only by price and that those customers could be profitably harvested under those terms. A supermarket chain was cited as a glittering example. Their outlets are the sort of vast, grey concrete hangers where sad people with snotty kids and fat arses waddle out with trolleys laden with Day-Glo orange and green soft drinks, 40lb bags of cheap chocolate marshmallows and twenty-four putty-coloured loaves of sliced bread. Too miserable and depressing to even contemplate owning a company like that. Yet, should you be so full of despair and lacking in joie de vivre that you open one of these places in competition, try throwing in a smile, a bit of service, some knowledgeable people, and you will scoop the pot. They do not realise how vulnerable they are. No one in their game has nice, happy, value-adding people, so they believe wrongly that you don't need them. Good people, your peasant army is the Trojan horse that will allow you to tear these walls down.

THOUGHT

If you are in a crap industry, just being consistently less crap than the competition will keep you ahead of the game.

DAI'S CRISP INVASION

Our idiot friend also suggests dumping unprofitable customers. A story may help you to think about that. A true story with the facts changed a little to protect the innocent, or more importantly, me. The country's biggest snack maker discovered that North Wales only ordered two boxes of potato crisps a week, and a huge truck was despatched to deliver them. Cost £500, receipts £15, therefore the trip was uneconomic. So, for a while, you couldn't buy potato crisps in North Wales. But there was a small local baker who could use £15, and who started making his own crisps. Oh boy, were they yummy. People came from miles around to buy these crisps. Soon his huge trucks were leaving North Wales laden with his scrummy product. The competition were crushed by his excellence. In the end he was brought out by one of the world's biggest fast food chains but there you go, at least Dai whatshisname trousered a few hundred million and bought his own tropical island, all because the original company was guided by blinkered economic advisors.

POINT
If you give your competitors just one foothold, they may just climb all over you.

YOUR PEOPLE'S ARMY

Airlines are just like the children's character Noddy, who said 'When we build a house, let's put the roof on first so when it rains we don't get wet.' Only the airlines are saying 'Those passengers pay two hundred pounds, and those pay two thousand. We will only carry the two-thousand-pound ones.' This is like sawing the legs off your chairs and expecting the seat to stay in the air. Where do they think big customers come from? They come from loyal small customers.

The world has truly changed, producing threats and opportunities. The mega-corporations can no longer expect to have it all their own way. By having loyal, even – dare I say – fanatical multi-tasked people working for you, and the whole world to source products from you, you can take on the biggest and win, but your customers will expect responsiveness and speed. Hierarchies just cannot work, people will expect a result whenever and wherever they contact our enterprise. Cheery, helpful, knowledgeable people who add value at every step. Without them, nothing works. I read about each management fad, TQM, CRM, Process Re-engineering, Excellence, Change programmes, or even Customer Care. The day I read the book I am sold on it, and then I watch as it fades and dies. Surely some of the ideas must have been good ones. There must have been some common fault. Perhaps none of them carried their people with them.

KNOW WHERE YOU ARE GOING AND TELL EVERYONE ELSE WHERE YOU ARE GOING. THEN YOU MUST EXPECT THEM TO HELP YOU GET THERE.

A SAD TALE

This story, I suppose, sums up the whole meaning (if there is one) of this book. You may remember that earlier I had said, in fairly dismal mood, that large companies can continue being indifferent to us because we can't be bothered to change. Well, let me tell you, my bank have just about done it. They are so frustratingly awful that I might just get off my arse and move my accounts. Some bright spark, high up in their organisation (but not the very top – I should think they have no idea what's going on) has had the consultants in, and they have decided that CRM is the way to go. However, the nasty, unruly, undisciplined customers won't play ball. The idea is that all calls will go to the Call Centre – be it in Bolton or Bangladesh. The skilful operator will deal with the customers' requests or divert them to a 'Centre for Excellence' (a branch, to you or me). The trouble is that the naughty old customer likes to ring their own personal branch (sorry, Centre for Excellence) and chew the fat, have a chat with big Beryl, ask certain unpredictable questions. The truth is that customers, when given the option, always ring the branch. Well, it's just not good enough and it has to be stopped. Although all trace of direct numbers have been taken from directories, sneaky customers are still finding them out. Verily, an edict was passed that any member of staff revealing direct contact details would be disciplined. Give me strength. The other day, I had a business trip to Rubovia or some such weird place, and I needed some Rubovian Copeniks. Normally I ring the branch's foreign exchange desk, and give them 48 hours notice if I need some bizarre foreign currency. Not this time. I rang the Call Centre. No, I couldn't have the branch number. No, I couldn't be put through to the branch. Did I have my password, sort code, which account was the foreign exchange to be made through? It drove me nuts. You can't make appointments because you can't discuss who is the best person to make the appointment with, and when I started to whinge at the branch, they stopped me mid-whinge. 'We know you are going to complain about our CRM, well let us tell you, we really hate it. Do you know, we even had a precise plan and picture of how to decorate the corporate Christmas tree.' I asked if I could pass my complaint up the chain of command. 'No, if you write to Head Office, they pass the letter, virtually unread, to us because the Centre for Excellence is "empowered" to deal with it.'

ABANDON SHIP

There you have it, a supertanker heading for the rocks. The passengers waiting patiently in the lifeboats, the crew are all wearing their lifejackets, and there is a focus group on the still blissfully ignorant bridge. Arrogance, unarmed peasants, pissed off and powerless customers, restricted access to most parts of the company – all consultant-driven gobbledegook. A giant that is vulnerable to your dagger of intelligence. After reading this book, examine this bank experience and think how you would be able to do it better.

THE WORLD'S YOUR OYSTER

One of our biggest supermarket chains was crowing about how clever it is at kicking the crap out of the competition. Maybe, but the signs of trouble are there. The once fresh 'fresh orange juice' is now, in small print, pasteurised 'fresh orange juice'. And it doesn't taste as good. They also claim to be getting on top of internet grocery shopping and are held up as a glittering example, but I was discussing this with a student of commerce, who told me that they succeed by distributing from store and warehouse. There is a fear amongst consumers that you may get the bruised fruit, or the stuff that is close to its sell by date. No worries though, their obvious competitors don't come close, but what of their not so obvious competitors? You could be flogging caviar and smoked salmon from your garage, rare Chinese mushrooms from your shed, or really fresh fresh orange juice from your cold room. The danger for the big boys is you. Marketing is showing this. The big TV advertising campaigns are dying, the big newspaper campaigns are on their arses, the market is fragmenting.

I have a rare pinball machine that needed parts and found on the Internet kind, helpful people at a company called Pinball Heaven, who supplied every part I needed with a smile.

The paradox is that on one hand you have the huge global market that makes the world small, but this has caused fragmentation that for the smaller, faster, focused and more flexible enterprise makes the market huge.

I hope you enjoyed my mad scrawlings and may they bring you the riches *you* desire.

MAKE IT ANYWHERE, SELL IT ANYWHERE.

- *Arm your peasants.*
- *Listen to your customers.*
- *Offer outrageously good service.*
- *Build loyal customers.*
- *Don't employ anyone you don't trust; otherwise put trust in your people.*
- *Let people make money for you.*
- *Go for outcome, not process.*
- *Have fun.*
- *Let everyone else (your people, your customers) have fun.*

Cheerio and best wishes.

Geoff Burch

INDEX